W

The Goddess

WAY *of*
The Goddess

Ann-Marie Gallagher

Thorsons

Thorsons
An Imprint of HarperCollins*Publishers*
77–85 Fulham Palace Road
Hammersmith, London W6 8JB

The Thorsons website address is: www.thorsons.com

and *Thorsons*
are trademarks of
HarperCollins*Publishers* Limited.

Published by Thorsons 2002

1 3 5 7 9 10 8 6 4 2

© Ann-Marie Gallagher 2002

Ann-Marie Gallagher asserts the moral right to
be identified as the author of this work

A catalogue record for this book
is available from the British Library

ISBN 0 00 711787 6

Printed and bound in Great Britain by
Martins The Printers Limited, Berwick upon Tweed

Contents

INTRODUCTION

This book is for those who want to know more about Goddess spirituality. It describes and discusses contemporary Goddess beliefs and practices and provides exercises in every chapter for readers to try out for themselves. It offers a glimpse into the historical background of the present-day revival, and looks at the ways in which the Goddess still speaks to us in the twenty-first century. Within these pages you will find examples of and explanations for the rituals that the Goddess community perform to celebrate the Goddess, the seasons and the cycle of our own lives. To those of you for whom this is a first step on the path, many blessings on your journey!

WHAT IS
Goddess
Spirituality?

Goddess spirituality is a joyful, celebratory path that honours the divine as female. Those who follow this tradition honour a Goddess of inspiration, healing, friendship, justice and compassion. She is seen as both one and many, and we honour Her in all Her aspects. Goddess-spirituality reveres both human and non-human nature as sacred and heals the old divisions between mind, body and spirit. It is a 'holistic' path, which sees all existence as interconnected. It is an inclusive path: that is to say that it is open to all who are willing to step into that life-affirming space we call 'Goddess consciousness'. It welcomes all, regardless of class, gender, disability, ethnicity, or sexual orientation. It is a path that has particular relevance to women, but is also inclusive of men.

The Goddess tradition is a natural spirituality; it honours and reveres all nature as sacred. We follow the changing of the seasons and mark them with celebrations and rituals. In our festivals, eight in the year, we commemorate different aspects of the Goddess as the seasons pass. We also mark the seasons of our own lives, in rites of passage that help us positively value the processes of birth, growth, maturing and ageing to which we are all subject.

Having a Goddess at the centre of our spiritual practices means having to look at the world in a different way from that offered by religions with a male God at their centre. It also entails looking differently at spirituality itself. Having a Goddess means incorporating practices that have, for millennia, been ascribed to women and 'femaleness' and subsequently disregarded as unimportant. A good example of this is the skill of building and maintaining relationships. Because of patriarchy (rule of the fathers), women have been socialized into being relational, sympathetic negotiators of connections within and between families, communities and neighbourhoods. In a Goddess-centred spirituality, this way of 'connecting' things together is prized and valued, and reflected in many of our traditions, including the notion that all existence, all living things, are interconnected.

The emphasis on connection rather than separation means that our Goddess is not seen as separate from all creation, or above and superior to it. Neither is She 'the boss', in charge of us all, or the Supreme Authority. Our Goddess is someone we can call upon, a friend. We see and experience Her presence in all of creation — including ourselves. This is rather different from some of the ideas of male Gods that have predominated in the west over the last few thousand years. Accordingly, the Goddess is an entirely different concept, not just God in drag!

Our spirituality is distinctive in that we honour and celebrate the material world — the here and now. We consider that all existence is sacred, and that all things in the material world have spirit. In turn, spirit is not elevated above the material world, as has happened in many God- and male-centred cultures, but is seen as equal with and part of it. The idea that mind, body and spirit are separate and that the spiritual and mental faculties are superior to, and separable from, the body, is relatively new in human history. Our spirituality blurs these false boundaries between the mind, body and spirit and heals a breach set in place by philosophies that denigrated the physical world as 'base' or 'dirty'. In the past, the association between women and nature has meant that women have been seen as part of 'base' physicality. Our allegedly 'animalistic' nature, manifest in menstruation, pregnancy, childbirth and lactation, placed us, within this divided thinking, closer to nature in its most derogatory sense. Consequently, women have, at times in the recent past, become seen as less spiritual than men. Goddess spirituality does not recognize this division, let alone the negative connotations that are directed towards women, animals and the rest of nature.

Many of us are very interested in the history and pre-history of Goddess worship, mainly as a way of acknowledging and affirming the importance of a divine female figure in past contexts. Her importance and meaning to past societies have until relatively recently been disregarded by successive generations of archaeologists and historians. Sadly, social assumptions about gender roles affected the ways that artefacts and texts have been interpreted by a number of academics, who relegated the female figurines and Goddesses of recovered religious texts to the role of fertility symbols or wives to more important male Gods. In fact, there is a great deal of evidence to suggest that ancient Goddesses represented far more than human reproduction. Many female deities were credited with the invention of writing and language, for example Nidabar in Sumer and Sarasvati in India.[1] The patroness of mathematics in classical Greece was the Goddess Athena, and the Parthenon, built in her honour, is an architectural paean to the art of mathematics and geometry, the development of which is accredited to Her. Goddesses of knowledge, wisdom and judgement also abound in the ancient world; these include Ceridwen in Wales, Brighid in Ireland, and Maat in Egypt. Isis was invoked not only as All Mother, but also as a great magician and healer. It is clear, from the range of functions that the Goddess was seen to serve at different times and in different locations, that the figures and texts referring to Goddesses could not have been directed towards a deity that was simply, and reductively, a 'fertility symbol'.

The history and prehistory of the Goddess and the meaning of her cultural presence in a number of societies and locations on the planet is still being discovered and debated. It is a presence that has been with us for some 27,000 years — possibly more. Today, seeing past images of Her and reading past invocations to Her are profoundly inspiring and, for many women, positive affirmations of ourselves as women. This is why, although our spirituality is very contemporary and 'real-world', we occasionally look over our shoulders to remind ourselves that the Goddess has been present in human society for a very long time. We do not claim a single, unbroken line of continuity back to ancient, Goddess-worshipping cultures, but we do acknowledge the continuity of Her presence in human cultures over nearly 30,000 years.

Although we draw inspiration from the Goddesses of ancient, Neolithic and even Palaeolithic cultures, we are a very contemporary movement. Our Goddess spirituality, community and practices are based upon creativity in its many forms. We draw strength from interrelatedness and co-operation. We are interested in power as it emerges from within, and is directed towards empowering others, not getting power *over* them. We draw upon ancient symbols and merge them with new ones to keep our spirituality relevant and grounded. We look into myths from the past to find the real Goddess hiding between the lines. We appropriate old stories, and create our own myths as a way of telling Her story in a way that is meaningful to us, Her people. So, although Goddess people (because that is who we are) keep watch for historical continuity, we are inventive participants in the unfolding story that is our spiritual path.

How Did it Evolve?

Present-day Goddess spirituality grew up out of two very different movements. These are the pagan movement, spearheaded in the first instance by Wicca, a mystery religion, and the feminist movement of the 1960s and 1970s. It was, to a certain extent, the crossing over of these movements that produced, or fed into, Goddess spirituality as we now know it. Although it evolved largely from contact made between the two movements, for some it was a straightforward road from women's liberation.

The growth of the Pagan movement began in Britain in 1951 with the repeal of the outmoded Witchcraft Act. When it became legal to practise witchcraft, Gerald Gardner published a book describing a religion known as Wicca, the 'religion of the witches'. Wicca involved reverence of both a God and Goddess, and was naturally attractive to women who had not hitherto experienced involvement with a female deity. Although Wicca was in many respects conservative about the matter of the respective roles of men and women, and of God and Goddess, the mere presence of a Goddess fostered interest in ancient Goddesses and the possibility of a meaningful Goddess presence in the modern world. The Pagan spirituality of the Wiccans offered a new relationship between humans and nature and also evoked an interest in ancient Pagan traditions. Pagan goddesses were found to be interesting, independent women, held in high regard, and without need of a male consort. Those intent on exploring this path in pursuit of Goddesses both ancient and modern were in for a pleasant surprise.

In the meantime, in Britain, Europe and the USA, from the late 1960s, a groundswell of protest against women's subordination in western societies and other societies around the world was taking place. Within this movement, consciousness was raised about the ways in which patriarchal society had oppressed women on all levels. Whilst women were busily discovering the extent of their oppression, it occurred to many that their inferior position in culture and society was experienced at the level of the religious and the spiritual. Whilst some women chose to reject the notion of religion and spirituality as automatically oppressive to women, others set about recovering their birthright as spiritual beings by building a woman-centred spirituality. This required a huge effort of will, creativity and energy, and a search for something on which women could build.

It was perhaps natural that these women should turn their attention to evidence of Goddess-revering cultures from the past for inspiration. It became clear, during the soul-examining of this era, that it was not only the institution of a male God that was the trouble, but the structures of religion itself. Instead of a set of rules that told you what to believe, what was right or wrong, and instilled guilt around sexuality or desire, what was needed was a spirituality whose expression began from within the self. In contrast to the culture of a Higher Authority at the top of a hierarchy that usually had women, children and people of colour at the bottom, Goddess spirituality would offer a 'flat' structure in which all were equal, all were celebrated and valued.

The Goddess movement really took off in the USA. Cross-fertilization occurred in the 1970s and 1980s between the growing Goddess movement and the Pagan movement, which had originated in Britain. Whereas the Pagan movement was not necessarily feminist at the outset, new ideas from the USA began to influence it. At the same time, the nature of the new writings and ideas about a Goddess-centred spirituality were taken up to a certain extent by people in the Pagan community on both sides of the Atlantic. This led to some lively debates within the Pagan community, and produced some interesting hybrid spiritual paths among the Goddess community. Contemporary Goddess spirituality came, to a certain extent, out of both developments.

Who Honours the Goddess Today?

Goddess people — people who place the Goddess, rather than a God and Goddess at the centre of their spirituality — come from all walks of life. We are teachers, academics, doctors, nurses, waiters, child-minders, students, counsellors and many other professions. We are working-class and middle-class, gay, straight, bisexual, male, female, transgendered, able-bodied and disabled. We differ in age and appearance, wealth and family background. In short, we have a habit of disguising ourselves as human beings!

There is nothing in our appearance that particularly marks us out as Goddess people, unless we happen to wear a pendant depicting a Goddess figurine or symbol, or a T-shirt with 'The Goddess is Fab — Official' printed on it in big letters. Because many of us are environmentally aware, we may veer towards wearing natural fabrics. Some, though not all, of us wear bright colours. This reflects our love of diversity, colour and vibrancy in all things. On the whole, however, you may only be able to identify us by talking to us.

In terms of lifestyle, this differs as much as appearance. Many Goddess people do like to have lots of Goddess images in their homes, mainly because we find this reaffirming and heartening in a world that disrespects the female form. Because we celebrate the material world and see it as being as valuable as, and concomitant with, the spiritual, we tend to be quite sensual — meaning that we value the senses we have. Accordingly, we may decorate our living spaces with natural fabrics and colours, rocks, stones, water, candles and incense. Many of us are environmentalists and become involved in campaigns against global destruction. This commitment is practised on an everyday level, too, as most of us are keen on recycling, using environmentally-friendly products and conserving energy. There is a high level of concern for animal welfare amongst us, and a consciousness that we have a responsibility towards animals as fellow beings. After all — we, too are animals. Accordingly, many of us are vegetarian or vegan.

We are a motley crew — and since we are also people who celebrate and honour differences, it is perhaps rather fitting that this is so. Collectively, the Goddess community is a colourful patchwork quilt, joined together by our creativity, pleasure in diversity, and love for the Goddess. It is a rainbow quilt, in which all the patches are equally part of an enduring and wonderful pattern.

Women and the Goddess

> *A woman raised in a patriarchal culture is told that she has the wrong type of body-mind to be taken seriously and to share a sexual sameness with God.*[2]

> *Goddess spirituality ... honors, affirms, and celebrates womanhood.*[3]

9

For women, the chance to enter the sacred space of the Goddess, where divinity is seen as female, can be a truly transformational experience. In the west, women, unaccustomed to seeing 'God' in our image, are busily reclaiming and rebuilding a tradition in which we see the Goddess as a beloved expression of our spirituality, and ourselves as the Goddess. This is a complete turn-around from the position in which women have been placed by patriarchal religions. The best they have been able to offer women by way of a female reference point has been Mary. Although the tales related to her are complex, the bottom line appears to be that she is honoured only as the vehicle for the ultimate Male spirit, and because she manifests extremely misogynistic ideals of womanhood; the impossible combination of Virgin Mother of Christ. Ultimately, Mary represents a role of deference and unquestioning obedience to the ultimate male authority.

Within Goddess spirituality, the Goddess is not held up as 'role model' to women, but seen as a symbol of endless possibility. She is many things, none of which are reductive or limited to the roles ascribed to women in patriarchal culture. We see Her at once as gentle, caring, nurturing, playful, creative, angry, energetic, pro-active — in fact all the things we find within ourselves. The very fact of a female face of divinity is in itself revolutionary as far as women in the west are concerned. In Her we see ourselves. In ourselves, we see Her. Because we value our bodies, and see spirit at one with matter, we do not separate 'God' from the Earthbody, or our own bodies. But for women to see ourselves at all in a male God requires that we deny our bodies and refer to a God-spirit, beyond gender and beyond the material. This entails seeing mind-body-spirit as separate, and denying our everyday experiences as women — denying *ourselves*. Goddess spirituality, however, offers women the possibility of the experience described by Ntozange Shenge; 'I found god in myself ... and I loved her fiercely.'[4]

The attraction that Goddess spirituality holds for women, then, is clear. Whether we consider ourselves feminist, or do not ascribe to any politicality at all, women are offered, within Goddess-space, the chance to *be*. But what about men? I have already stated that Goddess spirituality is inclusive, and that men are numbered among those who make up the Goddess community. As a woman, I would not presume to speculate on what Goddess spirituality offers men, simply on the grounds that I do not live as a man and experience what men experience in patriarchy. However, as one Goddess man vouchsafed; *It offers a totally different experience of spirituality, and a chance to get away from models of masculinity that promote male dominance*. This demonstrates that a spirituality with a Goddess at its centre is about more than simply changing the sex of God; the presence of a Goddess means rethinking the way that spirituality is 'being done'. For men, this difference in approach is perhaps what Goddess spirituality offers most to them.

For women, learning about the existence of ancient Goddesses can be both poignant and empowering. The fact that things have not always been as they are now encourages us in the belief that things can change, and change for the better. The knowledge that images of the Goddesses of past cultures have survived, helps us to believe in our own survival in a world that, by and large, is still hostile towards women. Although the Goddess of the past has been hidden and, at times, denied, She nonetheless speaks to us of a time when women could see themselves in Her image. The present-day growth of Goddess spirituality offers women a chance to recover this possibility, and to celebrate ourselves, and our femaleness.

Present-day Goddess spirituality is busy in the task of creating a new culture in which women are valued, and celebrated as whole and complete human beings. The Goddess is the symbol of this emergence of an inclusive and woman-friendly culture, and a mirror image of the beauty and strength that all women can find within themselves and in each other.

Different Approaches to Goddess Spirituality

Goddess spirituality is really an umbrella term for a range of different Goddess-centred paths that characterize contemporary reverence for the Goddess. Strictly speaking, these should include those spiritualities that refer to the Goddess, or Goddesses within their practices. This would include mainstream Wicca, which includes a God and Goddess, Hinduism, which has a whole pantheon of Gods and Goddesses, and elements of Paganism that honour a God and Goddess. However, the Goddess spirituality spoken of in this book refers specifically to traditions that honour an holistic Goddess; that is to say a Goddess that is not partnered with a male God or Gods. Even so, Goddess spirituality is a collective term for a number of different approaches to honouring the Goddess.

One of the major differences between groups within Goddess spirituality is the way that the Goddess is perceived. Some people prefer to see Her as an entity, not exactly separate from, but arising from material existence. Others see her as solely immanent — within human minds, spirits and bodies. Others still see her as manifest in the material world, of which we, too, are a part. Some Goddess people see Her as both immanent — within — and external — in the material world. For some, the Goddess is seen purely as a symbol of the interrelatedness of all life, and the spirit of connection. It is entirely possible in our patchwork quilt community to combine all of these beliefs and have at once an entity who is both immanent and external to the self, manifest in all existence and who functions as a symbol of our deep spirituality. There is no sense of contradiction in combining these different approaches, as we base our understandings of the spiritual on our own experiences.

It is a common misunderstanding that all Goddess-centred spiritualities are automatically feminist. Although many of us would describe ourselves as feminists, some of us would not. In fact, some strands within the tradition tend towards duplicating the social image of women as primarily, even exclusively, carers, birth-givers, nurturers and facilitators in their interpretation of the Goddess. The Goddess spirituality described in this book is feminist and liberatory, and looks at the many aspects of the Goddess, including ancient roles that have been neglected, and the developing modern roles that keep our spirituality fresh and ever-evolving.

It is important to note that, although Paganism in forms both ancient and modern, has to a certain extent informed the growth of Goddess spirituality, not all Goddess people identify as Pagan. Some Goddess people are working from within traditions into which they were born, or which they chose early on. Christian and Jewish Goddess people, for example, may attempt to reinterpret their religious traditions from within. This transformation of tradition has included, for them, experiencing God as female. The status of those seeking to reform traditions from within fulfils the criteria for being described as 'Goddess people'. The Goddess spirituality described within this book, however, describes a path that operates outside of structured, orthodox religions, and one that incorporates different aspects of Goddesses from various cultures and religious and spiritual traditions.

WAY of

Thealogy: Doing Spirituality Differently

One of the things that you will notice as you proceed through the book, is that Goddess spirituality is very different from what 'spirituality' has come to imply in the west. As well as transgressing traditions that have seen divinity as exclusively male, Goddess spirituality celebrates the whole of a human's being — not just the 'separated' spirit that has been elevated above, and to the detriment of, the body. In addition, we see the whole world as sacred and as part of the spiritual domain.

The study of the nature of the Goddess, or Goddesses, is known as thealogy. This term applies to our understanding of the Goddess, the physical and spiritual Universe, and our place in it. For many of us, thealogy also describes the way we interpret and act upon our spiritual understanding. Thealogy has been described by Carol P. Christ as a way of placing interpretations of a symbol (the Goddess) above explanations of it.[5] This is certainly one aspect of thealogy, and it describes very accurately the emphasis that Goddess spirituality places on personal experience in all its diversity. Another way of looking at thealogy is to see it as a way of negotiating our relationship with spirituality, and questioning what we mean when we use words such as 'sacred', 'divine', 'spiritual' and, of course 'Goddess'. To negotiate our approach to, and understanding of these on the basis of interpretation rather than explanation is really to 'do spirituality' differently.

There are many possibilities, then, that thealogy offers, including a relationship with the Goddess. For Goddess people, the Goddess is not remote, unapproachable, punitive or an all-powerful interventionist in the playing out of human history. Rather, She is a part of

us, as we are a part of Her. She is someone who soothes and comforts when we are feeling weak, and whom we can draw upon when
we need to be strong. She is not merely consolation, however; she
can be a confidante to whom we tell our troubles, and a friend who
is right there with us when we need Her. We can call upon Her for
compassion. But we can also draw from Her the power to rebel, to
say 'no' and mean it. In Her Gorgon form, when she is the wild-
woman, with hair of snakes and eyes of fire, we can even call upon
her anger to get us out of dangerous or unjust situations. I have
certainly called upon her for calm, clarity and powers of analysis
when my workload has been high and my troubles many! She is a
symbol of hope, invoked not only through our feelings, but also
through our thoughts.

Thealogy is a moral, as well as an emotional spiritual approach.
Because Goddess spirituality sees life as an interconnecting web, of
which we are all a part, we pay special attention to the possible
consequences of our actions. This great web of being draws all
existence together, and flattens out all hierarchies, political and spiritual. As we are all part of the whole, no being greater or less than
another, what affects one part of the web affects the whole web.
This means that an injury to one is an injury to all, and, as Melissa
Raphael puts it, 'love directed to one is love directed to the whole.'[6]
When we act, we do so in the knowledge that the action has far-
reaching consequences. Being conscious of the value of all beings,
and the interconnecting impulse that draws us towards this realization, helps us to act in a morally responsible way. To act morally is
to embody the Goddess.

Another aspect of thealogy is to actively *become* the Goddess. This
means taking on roles that have been proscribed to us within patriarchal culture. Throwing off prescriptive notions of 'femininity' and

'masculinity' and taking on the mantle of priest/ess, wild-wo/man, green wo/man is one of the ways in which Goddess people do this. Stripping away the negatives found in our surrounding culture involves rethinking our place in the natural world. Goddess spirituality sees humankind as a species that has recently impacted disproportionately and negatively on the ecosystem, of which it is but one part. Thealogical reflection on this situation does not result in the conclusion that humans are irrevocably evil destroyers, but sees that our active reintegration with nature is necessary in order to repair the damage. Seeing ourselves once more as part of the natural world helps us to resist being poured into moulds prepared for us within mainstream culture, to make moral choices, and so to embody the Goddess.

You may have noticed that the word 'worship' has not been used in relation to contemporary Goddess spirituality so far in this book. This is because, strictly speaking, this is not what we do. The term 'worship' implies praying to, placating or bargaining with a superior Being. We do not bow before the Goddess or 'worship' Her in this sense at all. Rather, we call upon the Goddess in order to find and name Her within ourselves, in the world around us. For us, the Goddess is not an object to be worshipped but a subject, an active agent. Within thealogy, the word Goddess can be seen as more verb than noun. Although naming is important, so are process, activity, action. Just as all things living are subject to change, so are we, and so is the Goddess. Our active agency in negotiating these changes can also, within thealogy, be seen as the Goddess.

Before Doing the Exercises in This Book ...

In the course of this book, you will encounter exercises that can range from thinking and making notes to home crafts. One of the things that you will be asked to do occasionally is a 'visualization'. This means spending some time on an inner journey, in which you close your eyes and imagine yourself in different places and situations. This is to help develop your intuition, and connect with different aspects of yourself, and the Goddess. You should ensure that you have peace and privacy for carrying these out, and have a notebook and pen standing by so that you can note down important symbols, or immediate impressions when you return from your inner journey.

You should read the guidance notes for a visualization at least twice before embarking on an exercise, so that you can direct yourself by memory. Although it is possible to pre-record the journey on cassette, and play it back to yourself as you make your 'journey', this does disturb spontaneity; the pace of your journey is not always predictable, and the experience of it will differ from person to person.

You should ensure that you always eat and drink something, however small, when you have finished a visualization; food and drink are very 'grounding', and are often used at the end of rituals not only for the chance for a group to do something communally, but also to bring everyone back 'down to earth'. The following visualization will introduce you to some techniques of relaxation and journeying that will help you with subsequent journeys.

WAY of

Exercise: The Pathways Visualization

The object of this visualization is to get you started on the path of Goddess spirituality. The visualization itself is very simple; you will choose the path that you are to take.

1   *Sit or lie down in a safe place where you will not be disturbed for at least thirty minutes. Close your eyes and concentrate on slowing your breathing, until you are quite relaxed and ready to begin.*

2   *Imagine you are deep within yourself, in a dark space where there is no light. The darkness is absolute, and you are absolutely still within it. Stay for a while.*

3   *When you are ready, observe ahead of you a pinpoint of light. It grows bigger as you watch, and you soon see that it is advancing towards you at great speed. The light is a meteor, hurtling across space, and the heat and light of it increase as it grows closer.*

4   *When impact occurs, you simply absorb the light and heat, and see the scene around you lighten.*

5   *You are standing, barefoot and naked, on a dried mud path at the bottom of a meadow. Step forward onto the grass, feeling the greenery beneath your feet and the scent of it*

*as you move forwards. It is a sunny day, and
all around the meadow are trees, and the air
is filled with birdsong. A gentle breeze urges
you forwards, towards the top of the meadow,
and the slope that marks the foot of a tall,
green mound.*

6   *When you reach the foot of the mound, you
notice that there are three paths; one that
veers left, around the hill, another that veers
right, around the hill, and a third that leads
over the top of the mound. Choose which one
you prefer, and set off along it.*

7   *Whichever path you take, when you reach the
other side of the hill, your path continues
into a valley, and you will follow the track
onwards. However, before you continue, look
back over your shoulder at where you have
come from. What do you see?*

8   *Continue moving ahead, where a veiled
woman waits for you. She may be young,
mature, or elderly, and She may greet you
first, or stay silent. Pay your respects and
wait to see what happens. If the woman
remains still and silent, tell Her who you are,
and ask Her for a sign that will help you on
your way as you set out on the path of
Goddess spirituality.*

9   *The woman may speak with you — in which case take careful note of what She tells you — or she may simply present you with a symbol. Whatever She does, thank Her.*

10   *The figure will fade into the background of the valley, and you are free to explore the terrain further, until you are ready to end your inner journey.*

11   *When you are ready, sit down on the pathway, and will the scenery around you to fade, until you are in darkness again.*

12   *Return to the space in which you are meditating, and stamp your feet on the ground to help you 'come back'. Before you eat and drink, note down in your diary or logbook what you saw when you looked over your shoulder, and make a note of what the Goddess told you or showed to you.*

13   *The significance of what you saw when you looked over your shoulder before approaching the Goddess, and the words or symbol that She gave to you may not be immediately clear to you. Don't be disheartened — the human mind is notoriously cryptic when offering itself clues to the guidance and messages to be found within ourselves. This is where the note-taking comes in handy — you will be able to return to your notes and impressions*

*as you continue on your journey, and the
meaning of the clues with which you are
presented along the way, will begin to unfold.*

Notes

1   Stone: 1976 found in Christ & Plaskcow, (eds):
    1992, pages 121—2.
2   Spretnak, 1992, page xiii.
3   Foltz, T in Griffin (ed), 2000, page 131.
4   Quoted in Christ, 1995, page 97.
5   Christ, 1978, in Christ and Plaskow, 1992, page
    279.
6   Raphael in Griffin, 2000, page 94.

TWO

WHO IS THE
Goddess?

The many different paths within Goddess spirituality provide a range of answers to this question. However, what all Goddess-centred people agree upon is that the Goddess is many things, and is a strong, autonomous woman who does not need a male partner God to define or legitimize her. Goddess people, who have the Goddess at the centre of their spirituality rather than as a female 'half' to complement a male 'half' of divinity, perceive the Goddess as 'all-encompassing'. This means that She incorporates into Her both male and female, black and white, gay and straight, disabled and able-bodied, and so forth.

The term 'incorporate' is of great importance here, as to 'incorporate' means to have *in the body*. As Goddess spirituality is a profoundly embodied (em-bodied) spirituality, this also tells us something of the nature of the Goddess. For many of us, the Goddess is not a spirit floating off in space, or a lofty being separated from the bother of having a body. Rather, She resides within the physical world, which in turn can also be seen as part of the Goddess. She can be perceived within the beauty of a mountain, the drama of a thunderstorm, the smile of a friend, or the growth of plants. She can also be seen *as* the mountain, the thunderstorm and the growing plants.

Many people mistake this way of understanding the Goddess as 'Earth worship'. This is a common misconception. Honouring the Goddess and seeing the planet as part of her is not the same as 'Earth worship'. Because we see nature as sacred, and as part of the Goddess, we do indeed revere nature, of which we are also a part. This is very different from 'worshipping the Earth'. For us, the term 'Goddess' is not just another way of referring to the Earth, or nature. Speaking of 'Mother Earth' in any case is not a new way of referring to the planet — concepts of the Earth as female, and of nature and women as being endlessly exploitable, have been present in western culture for over 500 years. Linking women and planet, and expressing this as a 'Goddess' — Mother Earth — has served neither women nor planet particularly well. When Goddess-centred people see the Earth as the Goddess, this does not mean that the Goddess is limited to being fertile, exploitable, fragile. It means that we see her as embodied within our physical planet — just as we see her as embodied within ourselves and in the Universe beyond our planet.

Our way of understanding the Goddess as 'all-encompassing' challenges the ways in which spirituality has 'been done' in recent human history. All-encompassing does not mean that She includes both 'good' and 'evil'. This particular problem has dogged male-God-centred religions for millennia. Our relationships with the Goddess are different from past human relationships with 'God', and so the question of whether She encompasses both 'good' and 'evil' is meaningless to us. Our Goddess is seen as *connection*. This means that we see her as the ties that bind us together in mutual support, love and kinship. 'Connection' also refers to the delicate web of the ecosystem, in which all things depend upon all other things within it. This is known as 'interdependence'. Recognizing the interdependence of all living things and its necessity to the survival of the planet is also to be aware of the Goddess, who *is* connection.

The notions of 'good' and 'evil' are abstract philosophies which for thealogy have no meaning, and for which thealogy has no use. Goddess-centred spirituality looks at causes and outcomes in the everyday world with a clear understanding of ways in which changes can be made and responsibilities be ascribed.

The idea of the Goddess *as* connection provides a different way of understanding 'God-ness'. Consider this: connection is something that is not separable from the things that go to make it up. For example, which part of a web is the 'connection'? It is made up of many single strands, some of which are woven together. The weaving is an action carried out on it in order to tie separate parts of it together. The connection exists, but does not have a separate physical existence from the material that goes to make the single strands. For many of us, this also describes the Goddess. She is real, and palpable, but cannot be experienced in one single part of existence that is separable from the rest. Within this understanding, there are no abstract ideas of 'good' and 'evil', nor any sense of the Goddess including bad things that happen as well as good. Since the Goddess is not the all-knowing, all-seeing, all-purposeful entity of Biblical proportions, She is not 'responsible' for all the bad things that happen. Goddess people see Her in an entirely different way. For us, the Goddess is right here with us, both in the physical world, and in the hope we place in the connections that draw us all together.

The Goddess that goes beyond our planet, and into the material worlds beyond, was celebrated in ancient texts in many forms. The Sumerian High Priestess Enheduanna celebrated Innanna as a moon Goddess, in the earliest piece of literature to be ascribed a named author:

> *Lady of all powers,*
> *In whom light appears,*
> *Radiant one*
> *Beloved of Heaven and Earth*[1]

There have been many other lunar Goddesses, such as the Roman Selene, the Greek Artemis and the Ethiopian Tanith. There have also been sun goddesses, such as Amaterasu in Japan, Sekhmet in Egypt and Sulis in Britain. The Welsh had a goddess of the stars, Arhianrod, who was said to live in a tower in the sky, and referred to the stars as 'the court of Don', a very ancient founder Goddess. Although later civilizations became used to referring to the sun as male and the moon as female, present-day Goddess people have reclaimed the Sun as 'Goddess'. Our galaxy was created as parts of its central star broke away to form planets, which were captured in its orbit and continue to revolve around it. It makes sense for us to see this original parent star as female — an entity that forms within itself, and produces, offspring. The sun, therefore, is also the Goddess, and the Earth Her daughter. The daughter, of course, is also the Goddess. Goddess people also see the darkness, and the space between and beyond the stars, and all of the primary elements that go to make up the Universe as the Goddess. We also see that original 'spark', the *connection* that set things off, and contributed to its evolution, as the Goddess. This is what is meant by 'all-encompassing'.

Goddess and Goddesses: One and Many

You may have noticed already that the term 'Goddess' is easily interchanged with the term 'Goddesses'. This is because Goddess spirituality is *polytheistic*, which means that we have many Goddesses. Having many does not prevent us referring to *the* Goddess in the singular, and neither does referring to *the* Goddess prevent us from celebrating different Goddesses. There is a saying among Goddess people, that *All Goddesses are One Goddess, but not all Goddesses are the same*. This sums up rather neatly the way that many Goddess people operate around the issue of the One and the Many. The fact that we can learn about, approach and honour different Goddesses, see them both as distinct from each other, and at the same time as different aspects of the Great Goddess, reflects the way that we see all creation. The Goddess-centred Universe is composed of many individual 'beings' (including rocks, plants, animals, bacteria) that are connected to make up the whole. The fact that we perceive Goddesses and Goddess in this way can be seen as a natural extension of this spiritual viewpoint.

One way in which to understand the ease with which Goddess people switch between one and the other, is to see 'the Goddess' as an overarching term to refer to all Goddesses. This view allows us to see various Goddesses as different aspects of this all-encompassing Great Goddess. At the same time, it also allows us to name this Great Goddess by the many names by which she has been known around the globe from age to age. This does not mean that Palaeolithic, Neolithic or ancient peoples had this same idea at all; their Goddesses may have been very localized deities for all we know. But this contemporary way of seeing the One as the Many provides us with a spirituality based on the experience of our modern world.

For some of us, particularly the more privileged, the coming of mass education and the internet in the west has given us access to knowledge about other cultures, both contemporary and past. Mainly because of archaeological finds, feminist scholarship and research, we now know far more about Goddesses from around the world than our counterparts of even 50 years ago. Incorporating into the Goddess the knowledge that we have gleaned from recent discoveries helps us to remember that the Goddess is not experienced as a monolithic, single being. Another consequence of seeing the

Goddess and Goddesses in this way is that it does not preclude us naming Her. We can be speaking to the Great Goddess directly as *the* Goddess and still address her as Athena, Brighid, Oya and so on. This means that we can give the Goddess her name, or names, when we address her. The ability to address the Goddess by name means that we keep our spirituality up close and personal!

The appropriation of Goddesses from different cultures, both past and present, is in no way meant to dishonour the original concept of that Goddess, or to instruct Her contemporary adherents in different cultures in how it 'should be done'. The intention is to honour, and 'reclaiming' the names and aspects of the Goddess in this way is done respectfully, and in acknowledgement that some people may see Her differently. One of the advantages of incorporating Goddesses from different cultures is that for many of us, this reflects the world as we experience it. Some of our western societies are multi-cultural, and are made up from many different ethnic groups. It would be rather odd, therefore, if a path that values inclusiveness, and encourages the use of experience as a guide to spiritual development, insisted on limiting our concept of the Goddess. There are white, black, Asian and Amerindian Goddesses, and Goddesses from many different ethnic origins to be found from around the world. Incorporating these Goddesses into our repertoire is a perfectly natural reflection of the world we find around us.

In spite of the array of Goddesses from different cultures around the globe, many Goddess people do their best to find out about traditions attached to the place they live, or come from. Our real-world spirituality encourages us to stay grounded, and find out more about the roots of our spiritual affinities, in history and in the land. Finding out about local deities, or the Goddesses honoured by the peoples who once lived where we now live, is a very valuable process.

Making contact with the spirit of the land around us is also a necessary part of a Goddess-centred approach. It is an approach that can be described as 'foot before boot' — in short, we need to get down to basics before we fly off around the globe selecting Goddesses when we have yet to make contact with the Goddess next door!

The Triple Goddess

In Goddess circles, there is a tradition of triads, or things being broken down into threes, particularly in relation to the grouping of Goddesses. The number three is associated with the Goddess for a variety of reasons.

Historically, Celtic cultures, tribal peoples of the west, who were also Goddess-revering for the main part, had a penchant for triads. Many of the patterns of knotwork bear this out, and the triskullion is, even today, the symbol of Mann, an ancient Celtic stronghold. The evidence of fairy tales, some of them remnants of much older stories handed down orally, tends to support the idea that in mainly oral cultures, placing things in threes was generally a good memory aid. Indeed, druidic thoughts on wisdom and knowledge were memorized as triads. Nowadays we might call this 'chunking information'. But the power of three had rather more significance than just as an aid to memory; Goddesses appear in threes in the later literature, and artefacts depict three-headed deities.

These clues, from a group of cultures that have left us with lots of evidence about past Goddess-worship in the west, indicate that the number three was considered important, and mystical. Its relationship to the Goddess in the past may be due to several factors. More than one commentator has noted that a downward-pointing triangle

29

resembles both the pubic area, the shape made by the ovaries with the womb, and that made by lines drawn between the breasts and the pubic area. These are all sites of reproduction, sexuality and nurturing, and considering the likelihood that our ancestors saw reproduction as the preserve of women, it is little wonder that the number three is seen to relate to women's mysteries. Given the importance of fertility in prehistoric and ancient societies, it is hardly surprising that triangles, triads and the number three became closely associated with ideas of the Goddess.

But these past ideas, or rather our interpretation of them, are not the only source of triplicity being associated with the Goddess. One such source is found in the phases of the moon, our understanding of which is derived from both modern and ancient sources. Although the division between sun Gods and moon Goddesses is a relatively recent imposition in the history of religion, many present-day Goddess people still like to see the moon as part of the face of the Goddess. It is a key aspect of Goddess-centred spirituality that we attune to natural cycles and experience the Goddess, too, in this way. In our observation of the lunar cycle, we see these changes happening more quickly and immediately than we do the cycles of the Earth and sun, and so we have a monthly reference point by which to celebrate different aspects of the Goddess. There are good reasons to suppose that ancient cultures might also have associated the moon with the Goddess. In a world that calculated time in cycles, rather than linearly, the next shortest cycle after the day is the month, or 'moon-th', meaning one cycle of the moon. This is also the time between the monthly courses of women. Additionally, a baby delivered at full-term would have grown through nine (three times three) lunar cycles, when the mother was not bleeding. It would not have been at all surprising, then, for the Goddess to be worshipped in her lunar aspect.

The phases of the moon are traditionally divided into three; the waxing, full and waning moon. These three phases are associated with corresponding aspects of the Goddess; the Maiden, the Mother and the Crone. Although some Goddess people vary this a little, some seeing four or even five aspects, this triad remains the most basic and commonly understood division of moon phases associated with the Goddess.

Within the triad, the first, growing phase of the moon is seen as the Maiden aspect. The term 'Maiden' here does not necessarily imply sexual inexperience. Rather, it refers to a state of autonomy and independence, of personal growth and integrity, freedom and wildness. There are many Maiden goddesses, including the fierce Artemis, whose hunting bow is seen in the waxing crescent of the moon, Athena, Goddess of, among other things, wisdom and learning, and Brighid, who is a fervent defender of the powerless, and honoured at the festival of Imbolc, the first signs of thaw after winter. The Maiden aspect of the Goddess is fiercely independent, and often a great ally in the defence of the powerless or underprivileged. As the moon waxes towards fullness, the principle of independence shifts towards that of maturity, and sexuality without pregnancy. This is where the phase known as the Maiden aspect segues into the more sexually potent phase of the next aspect.

When the moon reaches its full phase, it is seen as the Mother aspect of the Goddess. This implies sexuality combined with fertility, nurture and ripeness. The Mother Goddess is full-bellied, voluptuous and fruitful. She is usually seen as either pregnant, birthing or nursing a baby. Mother goddesses, or depictions that we would now understand in this way, were numerous in prehistory. Figures representing female fertility were around in cultures that existed 27,000 years ago. There are many Mother goddesses,

31

including Demeter, who the ancient Greeks revered as bringer of abundance and greenery to the Earth, Isis, whom the ancient Egyptians called the 'all-mother', and the Welsh Modron, meaning simply 'mother', who is honoured at the Autumnal Equinox, time of fruitfulness before the darker days. The Mother aspect of the Goddess is creative, gives birth to wisdom, brings thoughts into action and manifests whatever has been sown. She is nurturing and protective, generous and embracing. This aspect is seen as one which midwifes ideas and actions into maturity. As the fullness of the Mother moon decreases, the Goddess ages into the next aspect in the trilogy.

The waning moon, from the time of its decline up to and including Dark, or New Moon, is the domain of the Crone. She is seen as the older aspect of the Goddess, passing from fertility to wisdom of experience and intuition. The Crone is elderly, wrinkled and bony. She is seen variously as a wise grandmother, an elderly spinner, weaver and cutter, or sometimes as the Goddess who eases the path between life and death. The waning crescent moon is seen as Her sickle, and the Dark Moon the time of Her mysteries. Crone goddesses include Hecate, the Goddess of the witches, referred to in Shakespeare as 'triple Hecate', Baubo, whose wicked humour cheered the grieving Demeter by flashing Her genitals at Her, and the Irish Morrigan, who ushers the souls of the dead to the Otherworld.

This idea of the Triple Goddess is not particularly new, nor is it exhaustive of the ways in which the phases of the moon can depict different aspects of the Goddess. However, it is a popular concept among Goddess people, and one that certainly encourages us to look at the moon, and the cycles of our own lives, in an interesting way.

The Goddess of the Life-Cycle

Like all spiritual paths, Goddess spirituality has its favourite way of talking about major life events. Birth, growth, death and what happens after, are witnessed in the cycle of nature that we see around us. Goddess spirituality sees these processes in humans as being equally as natural.

Our ancestors, who were very much more in touch with the cycle of nature on a daily basis, year on year, began, around 13,000 years ago, to cultivate crops. Here, in the growth and cycle of the crops, was a symbol of the natural round of birth from the seed, growth from the earth, maturity, and death, with the cutting down of the crops. And here, too, was found the most wonderful symbol of rebirth, of regeneration after death; the continuation of the crop from the seeds of the plant that had been harvested. There is a great deal of evidence to indicate that in early cultures, there were Goddesses of agriculture. Given the associations between the female figurines that go back to 25000 BCE, and the conspicuous and visible fertility, birth-giving and nurturing qualities of women, it is hardly surprising that this is so. Just as women grew children in their wombs and nurtured them, so the Earth grew crops from the soil and nurtured humans.

That our ancestors had similar ideas about the death and rebirth of humans is found in the many burial barrows and long tombs of the agricultural period. Although archaeological opinion on the exact function of the barrows differs, Goddess people today choose to see in them a purposeful representation of a swollen womb, tunnels resembling birth passages, and vulva-like doorways and entrances. We sense in them an attempt to duplicate the life-cycle of the crops, or the growth of the seasons. Just as flowers and fruit die off, to

33

return the following season, and crops are harvested and seeds from them replanted, so the bones of the dead were placed into the Earth's womb, to be reborn among those they had left behind.

Nowadays, there are many views amongst us about what actually happens to humans after death. Some of us believe quite literally in reincarnation after death, whilst others tend to take the view that as everything in the Universe is recycled, we simply become one with the processes of life, death and rebirth. Our knowledge about ancient Goddesses and the rituals attached to the major biological rites of passage inspire all of us, however, to understand these mysteries as part of an eternal cycle, ruled over by the Goddess in her various aspects.

At birth, we are aided by the Old One, the Cailleach, who smoothes our passage from the womb to the outside world. We are protected by Brighid, also a midwife and a protector of women and children, and in one of Her aspects, the spirit of youth. Our physical growth and maturation are presided over by Demeter, the Earth goddess, and patron of corn and vegetation. In the myths of pre-Hellenic Goddesses, reclaimed from patriarchy and retold by Charlene Spretnak, Demeter is also a loving and protective mother. Patronesses of maturity include Aphrodite, Goddess of beauty, love and sexuality, and Athena, Goddess of wisdom and learning. Whilst one rules the sexual aspect of maturation, the other rules over the sphere of learning. Our later life-phase is ruled by Rhiannon, Lady of Tides, who is wise, just and balanced, and sometimes depicted by modern artists as a mature, post-menopausal woman. Elderhood is overseen ·by Hecate, again in her Cailleach aspect, as Crone and Washer at the Ford. She is seen in Goddess spirituality as a Death Goddess. This does not mean a Goddess that causes death, but one who represents the ending of life, and who again midwifes us into the realm of death, from life.

The list of Goddesses above is not comprehensive, and there are many different Goddesses who could be used to represent the different functions of the life-cycle. However, it is important to remember that this is seen very much in a cyclical way. Death is not seen as the full-stop at the end of a sentence. Rather, it is seen as a natural part of the cycle of our lives, and the life of nature. We tend not to see these things as pre-destined, but as things that we expect to happen at some time, and celebrate accordingly.

In addition to having Goddesses who represent different aspects of our life-cycle, in the Northern hemisphere we also have a way of seeing the life-cycle of the Goddess in the cycle of the year. One way of imagining the life-cycle of the Goddess is as a circle, without beginning and without ending. Superimposed on a circle representing the solar year (see Figure 1), we see that the various points of the year can correspond with different phases of life. Expressed mythologically, this can also be seen as the life-cycle of the triple Goddess.

In deepest winter, at the Winter Solstice, she gives birth to the Sun, who is also Herself. If we follow the life-cycle of this newborn Goddess, we see that as She matures from childhood to womanhood at Imbolc, the beginning of February, so the cold and darkness of winter lose their grip on the Earth. By the Spring Equinox, when darkness and light are equally balanced, and the hours of daylight are ready to outstrip those of darkness, she is a fully-grown woman, who conceives of the Sunchild to be born in the depths of winter. In May, her greenery bedecks the fields and forests, and the flowers of early summer bloom, along with her early pregnancy. Traditionally, in May, she takes a partner — male or female, in affirmation of the power of connection, life and sexuality. By the Summer Solstice, when the sun is at the height of its strength, and her swelling womb

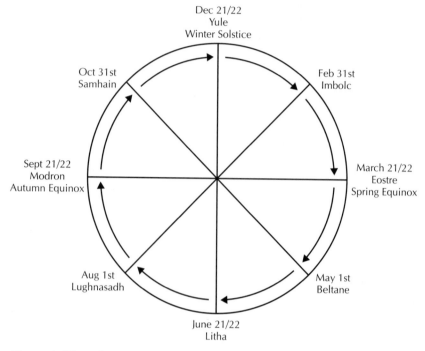

Figure 1: The solar year represents not just the changing of the seasons but the phases of life.

rises, the Goddess is in the full bloom of womanhood. At Lughnasadh, in early August, the corn crop is ripe, and she cuts down the corn, which is sacrificed to feed the people. Here, she meets her Elder Self, the Crone, who carries the sickle and reminds us to cut away that which cannot serve us unless it is removed. At the Autumn Equinox, when the fruits are ripe on the trees and summer is ending, She is in her sixth month of pregnancy, and as beautiful and ripe as the fruit that is ready to be plucked. As the greenery turns to russet and brown, She turns Her face to the West, the place of death, and remembers that the Dead, too, need her company. In Her compassion for all that was once living, and is now fallen, She sets sail across the western Ocean towards the Isles of the Blessed. In her absence, Her Elder Self, the Crone, begins to cull the vegetation, and at Samhain, the end of October, on the Feast of Ancestors, the Crone dances the Dance of the Dead with us, before going to the aid of Her divine Daughter, who is about to give birth to the new solar year.

These different life-phases, as you can see, overlap and intermingle. At the point at which the Goddess gives birth to her Younger Self, she is present in all three aspects; the Elder Self, who acts as mid-wife, the Mother who gives birth and lactates, and the Child, who will quickly become the Maiden as the days grow lighter. Just as the strength, light and heat of the sun aid growth on the earth, so the Goddess grows and matures. Seeing the mystery of the triple Goddess in this way helps us to appreciate the beauty and value of different phases of our life-cycle, and improves our understanding of the ever-changing nature of life, seen in the endless cycle of Earth's seasons.

Exercise: Meeting the Goddess of the Wheel

This exercise is designed to help you learn about the different phases of your life, and of yourself, using Goddess symbols. Carrying out this exercise will also help you to contact different aspects of the Goddess in the world around you, in your life, and within yourself. The exercise is a mixture of thinking, making notes and visualization. It is a good idea to keep a notebook beside you so that you can jot down notes of impressions, thoughts and visions as they happen. This is also a good way of beginning to recognize how powerful your intuition is, once you begin to trust and develop it.

1   *For this part of the exercise, you will need
a notebook and pen, and a quiet space where
you can meditate and concentrate undisturbed.*

2   *Take your pen and, in the notebook, draw
a large circle, and within it an equilateral
triangle. The points of the triangle will divide
the circle into three equal parts. Along the
outside of the triangle, but still within the
circle, write the following words, one along
each side: MAIDEN, MOTHER, CRONE.*

3   *Think about the characteristics of the three
different aspects of the Goddess that you have
read about so far, and write down, outside of
the circle, but close to each aspect, things that
you associate with that part of the life-cycle.
For example, you may find that you associate
the Crone aspect of the Goddess with wisdom,
wrinkles, grey hair, decay, death.*

4   *When you have finished writing as many
words as you can about each aspect, spend
some time thinking about the present phase in
your life, relative to the three descriptions of
the aspects of the Goddess. You may be in
your teens, and can be described, strictly
speaking, as being in the Maiden phase of
your life. Maybe you are a grandmother,
described as being in the Crone aspect? Even if
it is difficult to stick with one descriptor, try
to focus just on your age.*

5   *You will probably have found number 4 above quite difficult, as none of us are ever entirely one thing or another. For example, you may well be in your teens and have a partner, or have no partner and a baby. You may well be a grandmother who is both single, independent and sexually active. It is absolutely natural to struggle to stick with one aspect — you can, like the Goddess, be many at once! Write down which ones describe you right now, right next to the first one that you chose.*

6   *When you have finished thinking about the different aspects of yourself, start to think about the way in which these different aspects work for you in the course of one day. When you are in class, or at work, and learning something from an older or wiser colleague, you are perhaps using the Maiden aspect of yourself to receive information and make an independent judgement about what is useful knowledge. When offering your experience to a friend, or advising her, you may be drawing upon the Crone aspect of yourself. When offering to share your lunch with someone who has forgotten theirs, or finding a tissue for someone who is tearful, you are probably the Mother, nurturing, concerned, caring.*

7   *When you have worked your way through points 1 to 6, take a few moments to close*

39

your eyes, and contemplate the different aspects of Goddess within yourself. Do you have a name for each of them? Could you find their names by calling on them and asking them? How about researching these different types of Goddess, and hitting upon a name that seems appropriate to you?

8   *After you have meditated on this for a while, write down some notes to yourself in your notebook, to be acted upon later.*

9   *Make yourself comfortable, close your eyes and slow your breathing. Imagine that you are floating in dark space, without stars or any source of light. When you are completely still, both in body and mind, mentally draw a huge wheel in the dark, with eight spokes. It is lit with flaming torches at each point where the spoke meets the rim of the wheel.*

10 *You feel a presence close to you in the darkness. This presence does not show Her face, but directs you to watch the wheel, as it turns, endlessly. She explains that this wheel is the turning of the Universe, of the tides and the seasons, of all life, including yours.*

11 *Let Her speak on, and She will tell you more of the mystery of the wheel's turning.*

12   *When She finishes speaking, look back to the*
        turning wheel. Which spoke of the wheel are
        you on presently, in your life?

13   *Open your eyes and draw a circle, divided by*
        eight spokes, like the wheel in your visualization.
        Over the next week, think about the different
        phases of your life in relation to the eight points
        of the year described in the myth of the
        Goddesses' life-cycle above. Which point are you
        on right now? Which point have we reached in
        the seasons of the year in the world around us?

Keep your notes — they will come in handy when you return to
them later as they help to trace your personal and spiritual development, and provide guidance to the sometimes mysterious clues
and symbols that our sleeping, intuitive selves send to our waking,
conscious selves.

Personal, Social and Global

Another kind of 'wheel' that we use both to symbolize existence and
to find and understand our place in it, is the web symbol. The web,
like the wheel, has spokes that represent different places in our
lives, and places in the wider world in which we participate. The
web, however, combines the spiral, or eternally changing circle with
these spokes, and offers a map of existence and spirituality that is
at once complex and simple. The web symbol allows us to start from
ourselves, and move outwards to the social world and, from there,
to our place in the globe, and in the wider sense of existence; our
place and purpose in this life.

The exercise for Meeting the Goddess of the Wheel has already asked you to focus within, to look for different aspects of the triple Goddess within yourself. It has asked you to consider which phase of your life you have entered, and to ponder the different roles you play in the space of a day. The web symbol offers a way of extending this new understanding of yourself in relation to the world around you, to your relationship with others, to the planet, and to your life's purposes.

Goddess spirituality provides a great opportunity for looking within, and supports personal development in a number of ways. However, it is emphatically not for personal therapy only — it is a way of finding and acting upon our connections with the wider world in order to promote positive outcomes for all beings. The web represents the way that we begin with the self and move outwards towards the realm of the social (our relationships with others that we know, and with those we do not know) and then beyond, to the global.

Exercise: Visualizing the Web

This exercise is a visualization, so you will need to find a quiet place where you can lie down or sit comfortably and undisturbed for about 30 minutes.

1   *Close your eyes and concentrate on relaxing, and slowing your breathing. When you have achieved an even, gentle rhythm in your breathing, proceed with the following.*

2   *Take some time with this part of the exercise: imagine yourself sinking very slowly through*

*the chair, cushion or floor where you are
sitting or lying. Visualize yourself passing
through the floors of the building, then its
foundations, deep into the mud and rocks
below it. Continue slowly down into the dark,
passing underground lakes and rivers, and
sinking towards the heat at the centre of the
planet.*

3   *When you reach the red, orange and then white
hot centre of the Earth, and you are unable to
sink any further, begin to sink into yourself.
Imagine yourself travelling through the skin,
fat, veins and muscles of your own body, until
you hit the bones of your own skeleton.*

4   *When you are completely skeleton, you rise
out of your body, and travel back upwards
towards the surface of the Earth again. Upon
reaching the surface, you will notice that
everything has been pared down to its barest
structure, including all the animals and
humans, who are also living bones strung
together in the natural structure of their
skeletons.*

5   *High above the Earth, in a clear night sky,
the moon is now a silver wheel, the spokes
made from bleached white bones that emit a
powerful light. As the wheel spins, it produces
miles and miles of iridescent, silvery thread.
When you look closely, the thread runs*

between your bones to hold them together,
between yourself and the Earth, to keep you
from floating off the planet, between yourself
and all the other humans, and between all the
humans and all the animals. The thread joins
all humans and other animals to plants and
rocks, and to the air around and within our
skeleton forms.

6   As the spinning-wheel moon spins faster
    and faster, it begins to form the flesh on the
    skeletons, the leaves on the trees, and the
    feathers on the birds. It forms our hair, eyes
    and nails, talons, claws, fur, feathers, scales,
    and all the minerals, and the air we breathe.

7   Just as you are pondering all of this, you
    notice a loose thread, connected directly with
    the spinning wheel, and catch the end. It pulls
    you upwards, and you ascend rapidly above
    your neighbourhood, above the surrounding
    land, and above the continent. You are pulled
    out into space, even beyond the spinning-
    wheel moon, to a place where you can
    perch in something made of the thread, and
    resembling a hammock.

8   From your viewpoint in space, you can see
    that the whole of existence is made up from
    the threads of an enormous web whose
    proportions are both Universal and
    microcosmic. It is made of an infinitesimal

series of smaller webs, both forming and joining the smallest atom to the greatest body of matter.

9   *As you ponder this, you realize that the 'hammock' on which you are sitting is also part of the web — as are you.*

10   *When you are ready, concentrate again on your breathing, and return to the space in which you are sitting or lying down.*

11   *Before you get something to eat and drink in order to 'ground' you after your inner journey, take up your notebook and try writing down the answers to the following questions:*

- *What are the closest relationships in your life?*

- *What are the next closest relationships in your life, and what is the nature of them?*

- *Thinking about your relatives, friends and colleagues, what relationships do they have, with people that you both know and don't know?*

- *In what way are you related to the people connected with relatives, friends and colleagues, that you do not know and have not yet met?*

- *How would you describe your position in society?*

- *What is your relationship with others who do not share that position?*

- *How do your actions affect people you do not know and have never met?*

- *What space on the Universal web do you occupy and how can you affect things happening elsewhere on the web?*

12   *You should not be disheartened if you do not have exact or definitive answers; this is not a 'test', and only you can answer these for yourself. If you are unsatisfied with the answers you can provide at present, return to the exercise from time to time and try answering these questions again. Some answers may change, whilst others just make more sense as time passes, and you continue on your life journey.*

Notes

1   Enheduanna, *c.* 2300 BCE in Hirshfield, 1994, page 4.

THREE

GODDESSES IN the Twenty-First Century

One of the advantages that Goddess spirituality has in an age of technology and rationality is that it is a path that helps us to crack open, question and expose the conditions of our existence in a way that is unique among spiritual traditions. Our 'different', embodied spirituality helps us to explore reality in a way that gives credence to our everyday experiences. To see the modern world through the lens of Goddess-consciousness helps women in particular to reassess 'truths' that have been put forward, and the stories that have been told, not by, but about us and our place in the world. Finding the Goddess within and around us helps us to catch our spiritual bearings in an age that sometimes seems either totally devoid of spiritual integrity, or awash with 'fluffy' philosophies that see spirituality as separate from material reality.

But what, really, are the implications for a tradition that honours in the modern world a symbol that, prior to the middle of the last century, was consigned to the ancient and prehistoric past? Well, first and foremost, our Goddess, and indeed our Goddesses, have relevance as symbols in the modern world. You will be delighted to know that Goddess people are far too wise to be bound by the archaeologists' flawed interpretations of the roles and functions of Goddesses. Nor do we feel impelled to stick with the original significance of the Goddesses of past cultures in order to retain some sort of 'purity' of meaning attached to Her. We are creative people, and enjoy the freedom of invention inasmuch as it flows and blends with the principles of the Goddess of endless change. We are not Babylonians, Sumerians or Ancient Greeks, and so we must make our relationship with the Goddess as best we can; practical and adaptable in order that our spirituality remains 'real-world' and relevant.

Ancient and Modern: Creating the Right Blend

Many of the original functions of ancient and prehistorical Goddesses are still relevant, albeit in a different way. Reproduction, for existence, was considered far more important on a societal scale to our ancestors, for whom population was survival, than it is now to us in the west. This does not mean, however, that 'fertility' is unimportant to us on a physical level, or that it cannot be interpreted as taking different forms, for example, the creativity of the mind of a thinker, or the hands and skill of an artist, or cook. Ancient patronage by Goddesses of writing and language may no longer be in the same form; the original language over which She presided may now be virtually extinct. Our means of communication may themselves have changed; for example, they are no longer scratched out on a wax tablet with a stylus, written on a parchment with a quill pen, and presided over by a 'closed shop' of scribes or priests. But communication in the age of the information explosion is perhaps more important than it has ever been to us, and our understanding of the concept can be taken to include mass education, travel and telecommunications.

One of the ways of mediating the differences between the functions of ancient, named Goddesses, and their relevance to the modern world, is to blend ancient customs with modern interpretations. In this way, Athena, Goddess of wisdom, learning and writing, is an appropriate Goddess of all forms of communication. Given Her association with weaving, for instance, She is an ideal patron of the internet! There is absolutely nothing wrong or odd about this; appropriation and redefinition are part of the practice of a Goddess-centred spirituality. An eclectic approach, which means that we select symbols and associations from several sources and blend

49

them so that they make sense, is fully in the spirit of our tradition, which is itself both new, and old, and ever-evolving.

Another way of interpreting the relevance of ancient Goddesses is to take inspiration from ancient named deities, either about whom little is known, or whose cult or worship is inimical with present-day understandings of Goddess spirituality. Some Goddesses were either invented from within an oppressive patriarchal moral code, which gave them unpleasant functions, or were themselves appropriated from other cultures and given a job that fitted the rather unpleasant political agendas of the time. This is a way of 'rescuing' representations of the Goddess from their past, oppressive functions, and subverting the original, or distorted form with attributes that may be linked to her legends, myths or previous functions. Monica Wittig once declared:

> ... *there was a time when you were not a slave,*
> *remember that ... You say there are no words to*
> *describe this time, you say it does not exist. But*
> *remember. Make an effort to remember. Or, failing*
> *that, invent.*[1]

Goddess people take this quite literally, and gleefully permit ourselves to begin to tell our own stories, on our own authority, in order to recreate ourselves and provide a tradition for future generations to plunder and recreate for themselves! In this way, we aim to celebrate our spirituality and keep relevant the meaning of the Goddess to women and men in the contemporary world.

Goddesses for Today

There is nothing wrong in honouring the Goddess in some of Her more ancient aspects — this actually gives us a sense of our own history, in however an imperfect or incomplete way. However, thealogy differs markedly from theology in that it does not try to explain the Goddess in all Her aspects, but looks at the symbols that are offered to us to explore and interpret for ourselves. Accordingly, there is a strong impulse within Goddess spirituality to explore the relevance of different Goddesses in everyday life.

Some aspects of human existence are new and peculiar to our time, but others are perennial and part of the human condition. Using ancient names and functions that offer a thoroughly modern interpretation provides us with Goddesses of the office, the factory floor, the airport and the picket line. There are Goddesses that can provide comfort and strength for those living with AIDS and their supporters, or for those who are subject to substance abuse. For parents negotiating the dangers of modern life in order to protect their children, there are Goddesses of courage, protection and the everyday highs and lows of parenthood.

What is important is that among the array of Goddesses honoured within Goddess spirituality, it is possible to look at both traditional and modern associations, and explore for yourself the possibility of creativity, reinterpretation and, of course, invention.

WAY of

Brief Guide to Goddesses: Glossary, Associations and Symbols

The following is a concise glossary of some of the most popular and better-known Goddesses celebrated within contemporary Goddess spirituality. It must be stressed, however, that this list is neither definitive, nor complete — that would take several other books to achieve! However, the list of names, and their various functions, histories and interpretations, are a useful starting point for beginners. You can, of course, always follow up the names and descriptions of particular Goddesses with your own research: there is a list for further reading at the end of the book. A list of pointers is also useful when you are exploring a personal relationship with a particular Goddess, or aspect of the Goddess, and the exercise at the end of this chapter will help you to get that relationship off to a good start.

The descriptions, associations and symbols of Goddesses here are decidedly modern takes on their original roles, and are often a blend of their ancient functions and their contemporary meaning in the west, as described in the above sections. You should feel free to explore further the possibilities that arise from each description, and your own experience and personal encounter with, each deity.

Amaterasu   Sun goddess. She represents light in both its physical and metaphorical sense. Amaterasu shines light on hidden things, and is a protector against deception. One of her symbols is the mirror, which challenges us to look at ourselves clearly and honestly. She peels away masks and exposes folly and injustice. Origin: Japan.

Andraste   Earth Goddess. Andraste was the patron Goddess of Boudicca, who freed a hare — sacred to Andraste — prior to battle with the Romans. Andraste is protector of animals and woodland, an independent and fiercely protective Goddess. She has a fiery aspect when She is in defence of those who look to her for help. Her connection with animals and woodlands make her a natural choice, nowadays, as patron of those fighting against environmental disaster, and for animal rights. Origin: Ancient Britain.

Annis   Goddess of the travelling people, protector of the underprivileged. Also a Goddess of fortune, prophecy and herbal knowledge. Keeper of ancient wisdom, fierce defender of human rights and refugees. Annis is sometimes referred to as 'Black' Annis, and her symbols are variously the wheel, crossroads or road signs. Origin: Egypt, Nomadic.

Arhiannrod   Goddess of the stars, and the moon. Her symbol, the silver wheel, marks her as a spinning Goddess, and she is seen as the Goddess who spins the strands of the great web of all existence. She is seen as a Goddess of connections, magic, paradoxes and contradictions. Her mysteries can be solved with intelligence and intuition, and she is a good patron for those trying to find their way out of moral mazes. Arhiannrod offers guidance along the path to wisdom. Origin: Wales.

Artemis/Diana   Goddess of the waxing crescent moon, seen as her bow. She is popular with lesbian Goddess women and is a Goddess of great independence of spirit, and integrity. Some women-only spiritual groups are referred to as 'Dianic' as they honour this Goddess and keep company together in women's space. Diana was once a Goddess of childbirth, and today Goddess people celebrate Her in all her functions. Her symbols are the new waxing crescent moon, the hunting bow, and the She-bear. Origin: Greece, Italy.

Athena   Goddess of wisdom, learning, communication, science, writing, arts, crafts (specifically weaving), and intelligence. Athena is patron of clear thinking, and represents the ability to translate thoughts and ideas into action, and join thinking with intuition. She opens the door of the mind and the imagination to all of the possibilities of creative vision. She is also a protector of homes and a defender against aggression. Her symbol is the owl, and the equilateral triangle. She is closely associated with snakes and spirals. Although Hellenic myths made her into a cold Goddess of war, born out of Her father's head, she already had a long history as a Goddess of weaving and protection amongst the Minoans. The Romans appropriated the Greek Athena and gave her the name of Minerva within the Roman pantheon. Origins: Crete, the Peloponnese and Mycenae.

Aphrodite	Goddess of love, sexuality, beauty, the senses, romantic connection. Born out of the sea, she is also a sea Goddess, and rules the emotions. Her symbols are the rose, morning dew, myrtle and rosemary. She is closely associated with flowers and herbs, and with the scallop shell out of which She is often pictured emerging from the sea. Origins: Asia, Cyprus, Greece, Italy.
Astarte/Ishtar	Another Goddess of love and sexuality. She is associated with dance, beauty and allurement. She is also a primal mother Goddess and is associated with the heavens, as well as the earth. For modern women, Astarte is more than temptress; she represents the marriage of the spiritual and the sensual. Her symbols, appropriately, are the star and the serpent. Origin: Asia.
Baubo	Goddess of comedy and laughter. Having strong connections with the Sheelagh-na-Gig figures of Ireland, Baubo was the crone Goddess who exposed her vulva to Demeter, who was grieving for Persephone, and tried to relieve Her grief with laughter. Baubo is the anarchic, the unexpected and the disruptor of etiquette and false manners. Her laugh is a poke at authority, and a force to be reckoned with, as ridicule pointed at what is unjust or foolish can be a good way of beginning to strip it of its power. Baubo is the wise fool — the crazy old woman who has a method in Her divine and inspired madness. Her symbol is that of the Sheelagh-na-Gig — the exposed vulva, and

55

is used in households of Goddess people to ward off bad vibes and invite laughter and blessings into the home. Origins: Greece.

Bel/Sol

Goddess of the Sun. She is the patron of light, and warmth, of poetry and success in projects. She is also a deity of good health, and sometimes is connected with water, and healing springs. The prefix 'Bel' was often connected to solar deities, and means 'shining'. The Romano-British Goddess Belisama, whose name means 'shining one', was worshipped in Britain and Gaul, and at least one river in Britain — the river Ribble is named after Her. Bel represents both the sun in our solar system, and the inner sun, that gives joy and happiness to our own existence; She is the inner radiance that rubs off on others when they recognize a 'sunny' disposition. Bel's symbol is the sunburst. Origin: Britain and Northern Europe.

Brighid/Brigit

One of the most popular Goddesses in contemporary Goddess spirituality. Brighid is midwife, protector of women and children, healer, patron of smiths, and inspiration of poets; indeed all who produce objects of beauty. She is a fire deity, and her flower is the dandelion in its bright yellow phase. She has many healing springs and shrines in the British Isles, and one of her symbols is the serpent — ancient sign of healing knowledge. Brighid is celebrated at Imbolc, a women's festival held in late January/early February, when the first snowdrops emerge. She is a popular feminist choice as a patron, as she represents independence, integrity and protection of women, children and animals. Amongst Goddess people, Brighid has the reputation of lending Her fiery power whenever there is a need to stand up to authority and challenge convention. She is often depicted as a triple Goddess, with red hair and red or orange clothing. Origin: Ireland.

Bloddueuth
A Goddess of the springtime, and of flowers. She is the maiden built from flowers, herbs and tree branches, and is a kind of 'Green Woman' for late spring, early summer. Bloddueuth is portrayed as treacherous in Welsh myths, but contemporary Goddess people have returned to her function as spirit of vegetation and growth, which can be seen in the garden, the window box or the greenwood. Bloddueuth's symbol is a hoop of spring flowers. Origin: Wales.

Cassandra
Goddess of truth. She is the knowledge of truth within, and the voice of reason. Her voice is heard on the wind, in wind-chimes, flutes and wind instruments, jars, and in echoes. She is the patron of women who have been raped and disbelieved, and in her guise as Clio, the spirit of history. Cassandra is the spirit of stories and the hidden message in dreams. Origin: Greece, Africa.

Ceridwen
Ancient Goddess of wisdom and earth-magic. Very often portrayed as a crone or hag Goddess, Ceridwen is also a fertile earth-mother. Her

symbol is the primaeval cauldron, out of which life itself emerged. The cauldron is also said to hold a draught brewed by the Goddess, which bestows wisdom and great insight to any who drink from it. Welsh tales of Ceridwen's pursuit of Taliesen, who drank three drops from the cauldron, indicate her skill as a shape-shifter. Accordingly, she is seen as a Goddess of transformation and bringer of change. The Mabinogion, a book of Welsh mythology, gives us a clue to possible additional associations relevant to modern life: in the tale of Branwen, a magical cauldron has the power of restoring to life corpses that are placed in it. This reference to the cauldron symbol also makes Ceridwen an ideal patron of recycling and saving energy! Origin: Wales.

Danu/Anu

Ancient mother Goddess, possibly also a sun or fire deity originally, as her followers carried torches through the fields after dark in order to bring Danu's blessings upon their crops. Danu is Goddess of agriculture and food, and the earth's greenery. She is also a kindly protector against the fears we face in the hours of darkness, when human company and comfort are hard to find. Danu is a strong and loving protector, patron of creativity and consolation, bringer of light and comfort in the wee small hours, one who chases away our fears and bad dreams. Her symbol is a blazing torch. Origin: Ireland.

Demeter   Sometimes called 'Ceres', Demeter is a Goddess of crops and seasonal growth. She is seen as a mother Goddess who protects the seeds in the earth, and whose love for all growing things summons the shoots from the soil, and the earth to become fertile, green and fruitful. Demeter's symbol is a corn stalk. Demeter is seen as a loving parent who looks for her daughter Persephone when she goes missing. Many Goddess women see in her and Persephone's relationship — a relationship that is not celebrated elsewhere in patriarchy — the love between a mother and daughter. Demeter as bringer of joy, and as woman who sorrows for her child, is a potent and poignant symbol in a world where, in places, girl-children are still allowed to die because females are not valued. As Goddess of the greening of the Earth, Demeter is a natural source of inspiration for environmentalists. Origin: Egypt, Crete, Greece.

Eostre/Ostara   Fertility Goddess of the spring. Germanic in origin, Eostre is Goddess of the Northern Spring, and causes humans, animals, crops and vegetation to become fertile and fruitful. Nowadays she is also seen as the bringer of joy and blessings. Celebrated at the Spring Equinox, she gives her name to the Christian festival that covered the pagan rites of spring; Easter. Her name is also found in the word for the female hormone oestrogen. Nowadays, Her patronage of fertility can also be interpreted as the control that women need to

59

have over their own bodies in relation to fertility, contraception and sexual health. Eostre, therefore, is the ideal patron for the women's health movement. Eostre's symbol is the egg, the hare and the daffodil. Origin: Northern Europe.

Estanalahee   Goddess who brings fertility to the earth by dancing on the mountains. Originally an Amerindian deity, Estanalahee is honoured by women of all colours as a fertility Goddess. Here, the term fertility is extended to mean creativity in all its forms. She bestows blessings on those who labour to produce things of worth, true value and beauty, whether this is a loaf of bread, or a sand-sculpture. Estanalahee helps us see value in things that we take for granted, or that are disregarded in capitalist societies. She is the bringer forth of talent, creativity, fruitfulness, and helps us find wonder in simple things. In some tribes, She is also known as 'Changing Woman' or 'Painted Woman'. Origin: North America.

Fortuna   Originally an abstract reference to fortune and fate, Fortuna is nowadays honoured as the Goddess of fortune and change. She is also patron of the art of 'fortune-telling' and other predictive skills, making her Goddess of the tarot, palmistry, scrying (crystal ball or mirror-gazing), tea-leaf readings and astrology. Her symbol is the eight-spoked wheel. Origin: Italy.

Freyja The Scandinavian Goddess of love, sexuality and 'seidr' or seeing. Freyja is a powerful, energetic Goddess, who is transported through the sky on a chariot drawn by cats. Her necklace is thought to represent the source of all life — the vagina – and she represents full-blooded female sexuality. Drink spilt on the ground or hearth is dedicated to her, as she is also an earth and fertility deity. Origin: Northern Europe.

Frigg Often mistaken for Freyja, Frigg is in fact a Goddess who watches over the home, and all the domestic arts. She is patron of spinning, textile work and all the comforts of home. Frigg, like Freyja, is a 'seer', and represents the skills and arts of those who work in the home. Contemporary interpretations of Frigg place her as patron of homeworkers, who are most often women, and often exploited. Frigg celebrates the skills and arts that have in the past been dismissed and devalued as 'women's work' — whoever is doing it now! Origin: Northern Europe.

Gorgon/Medusa In patriarchal myths, the Gorgon is a woman changed into a creature with hair of live snakes, and of such monstrous visage that all who gaze upon her turn to stone. Contemporary Goddess spirituality sees her as the face of women's rage against injustices. The Gorgon reminds us that it is all right to be angry, that we are not being bad if we exhibit anger in the right way — that we are justified in feeling angry about a world that is

61

unjust. She is a source of life-saving strength, adrenalin and power. Some women have reported calling upon the Gorgon in times when they were in great danger, and drawing upon her power to fight back when attacked. She is also a potent symbol of protest against nuclear power and pollution. The symbol of the Gorgon is a shield embossed with her snake-haired face. Origin: Greece.

Grandmother Spider

Ancient earth Goddess who is now seen as Goddess of connection, transformation and wisdom. She represents intelligence and lateral thinking, storytelling and weaving. In the South Americas she is sometimes called Ts'its'tsi'nako — Thought Woman, and is seen as a creatrix, as she thinks existence into being. She has the power of naming, something removed from women in patriarchy, and translates thought into material manifestation. She has a link with language and ideas, and so joins creation of material things with the power of thought, intellect and feeling. Grandmother Spider is a crone Goddess, ancient and powerful. Navajo in origin, Her attributes are sometimes blended with those of Changing Woman, another Amerindian deity, as she is seen as a shape-shifter, and a catalyst for change. She is patron of crafts, including spinning, weaving, beading and pottery, and also of ritual and magic. Her symbols are the spider and the web. Origin: North America.

Habundia   Goddess of plenty. Habundia is a deity of material wealth and health, wealth here being in the sense of having enough food, shelter, care, etc to be comfortable. She is often depicted as a cornucopia — or horn of plenty, replete with fruit and flowers. The emphasis here is on need, not greed, and Habundia is a harvest Goddess invoked not only for individual need, but the needs of communities all around the globe. Origin: Europe, North America.

Hathor   Sun Goddess, and bringer of rains. Depicted with the disc of the sun between cow horns worn on her head, Hathor is a solar Goddess, who also represents earth/sky connections. She brings the inundation that makes the earth fertile, and is the sun who warms the sleeping earth. Where Hathor leads, light and life follow. Her symbols are the sun-disc between cow horns, and she is sometimes depicted in her sacred colours — red and turquoise. Origin: Egypt.

Hecate   The Goddess of witches, magic and the night. Hecate is a crone deity, who, like Freyja, is reputedly drawn through the air on a chariot pulled by cats. She is associated with cats, bats, moths and nocturnal creatures. She is the Goddess of the crossroads, who watches over travellers, and over those who have important decisions to make. Hecate is a weaver of wisdom, and is good to call upon when you need to achieve something without confrontation. If a battle needs to be fought, however, Hecate symbolizes the deep power we need to call upon for courage and will. Because of her modern association with witchcraft, she is often given the symbols of cauldron and broom-stick. Mistress of magic, herbal and anatomical knowledge, Hecate is a healer. Hecate is a midwife who sees over our birthing into the world, and our passage from life into death. Origin: Greece.

Helen of the Ways

A deity of obscure origins, who is today invoked as a Goddess of communication. She is some-times invoked by travellers and those who have lost their way, actually and metaphorically. Helen is a Goddess of the road and of the wayside. Her symbol is the crossroads and the stile. Nowadays, she is also called upon when electronic means of communication go wrong; for example comput-ers, faxes and photocopiers — making her an ideal Goddess for the office! She is a patron Goddess of lost things, and is often envisaged as dressed in yellow — symbol of the element of air and communication. Her symbols are those of a female Hermes — winged sandals and the planet Mercury. Origin: Possibly Welsh.

Innanna

Goddess of the heavens and the underworld, into which she goes every year. Innanna is the first Goddess to be celebrated in writing by a named author — indeed, the High Priestess Enheduanna's 'Hymn to Innanna' is the oldest text in the world to have an identified author. Today, Innanna is seen as a moon goddess, and an earth deity. She is seen as bringer of knowledge, wisdom and justice, keeper of history and ancient texts. Innanna is active, independent and a source of energy borne out of knowledge of the past. She is a natural choice for activists and those who fight for women's rights. Origin: Sumer, Asia.

Iris

Goddess of the rainbow, and of coalition and co-operation. She is a Goddess beloved in the gay community, because another name for Her flower symbol is the 'flag' — the rainbow flag is an emblem of gay and lesbian pride, tolerance and acceptance. She is a Goddess of quilting, of art, creativity and colour. Origin: Greece.

Isis

One of the most beloved deities in the contemporary Goddess movement, Isis is addressed often as 'All Mother'. She is seen as a mother, lover, sister and mighty magician. She is Goddess of the milky way, the sky and the earth and, in some traditions, is also a Goddess who receives the dead. She represents fertility, nurture and magical power. The ancient Egyptians credited Isis with the creation of written and spoken language, and she is seen as the Goddess who first gave power to words of magic. Isis is a creator and healer, and her symbol is either a throne or chair, and her colour the lapis lazuli blue later adopted by artists to symbolize the Virgin Mary — another celestial mother figure. Sometimes seen with wings, Isis is a moon and sky Goddess, whose nursing milk was, in myth, turned into stars. Origin: Egypt.

Juno

Originally a Roman Goddess of marriage and patron of matrons, Juno is celebrated today as a patron of relationships, including partnership and friendship. She brings blessing to parenthood, the home, and is Goddess of happiness and generosity. Her symbol is the peacock feather. Origin: Italy.

Kali

Kali is celebrated differently in several different spiritual paths, in different ways, including Hinduism and the Raddha Krishna sect. In contemporary Goddess spirituality, Kali is a Goddess of the life force, and represents specifically female energy in the Universe. Kali dances the dance of creation, and also has the ability to destroy and cut away that which is not needful, or is hurtful or unjust. She is an independent and fiery Goddess, who helps to channel righteous anger into just action. Kali is also seen as a fierce, angry and protective mother. Sometimes Kali is seen as the guardian of the 'place between the worlds' that we enter in ritual, or when we cross over from our conscious to our unconscious selves. Kali has become, like the misunderstood Gorgon, a positive symbol of feminist spirituality and direct action. Origin: Southern India.

Kuan Yin

Although originally, strictly speaking, a boddhisatava, Kuan Yin is seen by contemporary Goddess people as the Goddess of Compassion. (A boddhisatava is a spiritually advanced being who halts their journey to Nirvana in order to benefit humankind.) She represents consolation and mercy for those who suffer, and is often called upon when someone is sick, in pain, or suffering bereavement. Kuan Yin has been described by Goddess women as 'the place to go when there is nowhere left to go', and so is popularly invoked when things seem hopeless. Kuan Yin is a wonderful symbol of the tenderness that we need to extend towards others — and ourselves. She is a Goddess who is good to call upon when self-esteem due to trauma, damage or an emotionally deprived upbringing threaten to make us sick. She helps us to value and care for ourselves as well as others. Kuan Yin is a beloved figure, and symbols of her mercy vary. One symbol, however, is a teardrop of milk. Origin: China, Tibet, South-East Asia.

Laxmi   A Goddess of good fortune and wealth, and the success of independent and family enterprises. In India, and in Hindu communities around the world, she is celebrated at Diwali, the Festival of Light. Laxmi's patronage of good fortune makes her a Goddess of the fertility of enterprise, as well as of farms and other concerns. Her symbol is the lamp. Origin: India.

Lilith   A great favourite with feminist Goddess people, Lilith has her origins in ancient Hebrew mythology. In apocryphal tales of the creation, Lilith was Adam's first wife, who left him because she refused to lie beneath him in the act of sexual intercourse. For contemporary feminists, Lilith is

67

a symbol of liberation and independence. She guards over women in childbirth, and is a great friend to women who suffer injustice at the hands of men. She is a moon deity, though she represents the dark side of the moon. She rules over women's monthly bleeding, and is seen as a guardian of women's mysteries. For some, Lilith is an avenger, as well as a defender of women and children. Her false relegation to the annals of Jewish demonography, as a demon who steals newborn babies, also make her a good Goddess to appeal to when combating defamation and misrepresentation. Lilith's symbol is the disc of the moon, with one half white, the other black. Origin: North Africa.

Macha

Goddess of pregnancy, fierce righter of wrongs and wild spirit of dreams. In Irish mythology, Macha perishes giving birth to twins after being forced to run a race with horses by a boastful husband. Contemporary Goddess people honour Macha as a bold, independent Goddess of dark aspect, whose wildness is channelled in the cause of justice, and whose considerable powers to get the attention of those who abuse women and children are deeply respected. Macha rides the storm, and summons the brave to battle against injustice. Macha's symbol is the grey mare (or 'night-mare'). Origin: Ireland.

Maia

Goddess of the spring, and of flowers. Maia represents girlhood and early womanhood, and represents innocence, not necessarily as sexual inexperience, but as delight in worldly things without cynicism. She is often depicted with a circlet of flowers in Her hair. Because of Her association with youth and innocence, survivors of rape turn to Her in order to rediscover their trusting selves after trauma and injury. Maia is beloved of the contemporary Goddess spirituality movement, because She represents the peace to be found in creativity, and playfulness without being thought childish or child-like. Her symbol is May blossom. Origin: Italy.

Mare

An earth- and sea-Goddess. Mare is the spirit of nature, seen variously as Marion-in-the-Green, Queen of the May and Stella Maris — Star of the Ocean. Mare is rounded, fertile nature, the primaeval mother and the faithful sister. Mare represents the beauty and wonder of the material world, and the joy of spiritual connection with it. Her symbols include the drum, May blossom, and sea shells. Origin: British Isles, Northern Europe and North America.

Modron

Goddess of the autumnal equinox, and the fruit harvest. Her name means simply 'mother', and She also symbolizes the love between mother and child. She is seen as an apple-Goddess, whose maturity and ripeness reveals the mystery of beginnings and growth. Cut horizontally, the apple reveals the five-pointed star of the elements of all life within. Modron reveals the secret of the seed within the fruit, and at the height of her powers in the season of fruitfulness, She reminds us that even as the fruit is plucked, the seeds are ready for new growth. This applies to the nature of our existence, and the nature of change at an everyday level. Modron is the symbol of unending change and the promise of renewal and regeneration. Her symbols are generally fruit — grapes or apples. Origin: Wales.

Morrigan

The crow Goddess with knowledge of death's mysteries. The Morrigan was originally a dark aspect of a triple Goddess who presided over a region of Ireland. Nowadays, She is honoured as a Goddess who helps us to deal with the macabre, with fears of our own mortality, and to understand the nature of death itself, that comes to all things. Her symbol, the crow, is most apt, as it is a bird of carrion who has the reputation of feeding upon animal and human corpses. Morrigan is a symbol of the basic fact of our mortality, and the mysteries of the dark night. She protects us when we experience depression, doubts and fear, but does not shield us from the truth of our human and, therefore, mortal condition. She is honoured at Samhain (Hallowe'en), the day of the dead, and ushers the spirits of the ancestors to the feast. Origin: Ireland.

Nemesis

Nemesis is a Goddess of truth and reparation. She awaits those who behave badly or foolishly. Nemesis can be called upon both to help us understand our own flaws, or to pursue those who cause damage to others, and make them face the consequences of their behaviour. She is a good friend to call upon when you are magically binding a harm-doer, or seeking out the truth about bad situations. Sometimes depicted with eyes of black, Nemesis can absorb the slightest glimmer of truth even in situations that seem unfathomable. She is a Goddess that one should invoke in genuine need. Her symbol is the mask or the lantern. Origin: Greece.

Nephthys

Goddess of sisterhood, magic and mystery and darkness, childbirth and nursing. She is a kindly welcomer of the dead, and spreads Her protective and loving wings over women and their babies at birth and throughout nursing. She is a Goddess of sisterhood and solidarity between women, a role which is taken from the ancient Egyptian texts which describe her part in rescuing Osiris, along with Her sister, Isis. Nephthys is also a Goddess of planning and the secrecy necessary to protect others. Her role as magician makes her a popular deity with witches, as well as other magicians. Nephthys's symbol is the kite (bird). Origin: Egypt.

Nut

Goddess of the night-sky, in whose body the stars are set. For contemporary Goddess people, Nut is an expression of the Goddess of space, and the birth of galaxies. She makes the connection between this world, and existence beyond our planet. She is seen as a Goddess of beauty, protection and connection. Her symbol is the night-sky. Origin: Egypt.

Oya

Fierce Goddess of protection. Oya is a fiery-tempered Goddess, whose African origins were as a Goddess of Lightning, who warned against floods. She is popular in the Goddess movement as one who gives clear warning, and who has little patience with wrong-doers. She is often invoked against bullying and harassment, and to turn back the results of bad behaviour onto the originator of bad deeds. She is associated with the planet Mars, and the colour red. Her symbol is lightning, and a copper shield. Origin: Africa.

Pele

Goddess of volcanoes and fire. Pele is a real mover and shaker, and a good Goddess to invoke when you need to shake yourself or someone else out of complacency. She manifests in the form of action, and any situation that needs to be shaken out of stagnation or impasse would benefit from Her ministrations. Pele is a catalyst for change and illumination. Her unstoppable natural forces translate in magical terms into the bringing of realization and understanding to people who have deceived themselves that all is well. As such, She is an ideal patron of activists and protesters for change everywhere. Just as in nature, a volcano releases the deep, unstoppable forces of heat, steam and pressure, in a way that can change forever the landscape, in spiritual terms, Pele can channel our yearning, justifiable anger and visions in a way that brings social and cultural change for the better. Her symbol is a volcano, her colours orange and red. Origins: Hawaii.

Persephone/ Kore: also Prosperine

A daughter aspect of the Goddess, Persephone is also seen as a Goddess in Her own right. Persephone is both youthful aspect of springtime, and maturing woman, who through compassion chooses to go into the twilight between the worlds of the dead and of the living in order to comfort the recently dead. Accordingly, She is seen as both Queen of new life, and of death. Her relationship with Her mother, Demeter, marks Her as an independent and loving daughter — an aspect of Her that provides a symbol of hope for mothers and daughters in their struggle to make a valuable and meaningful relationship in a world that undervalues women and their relationships. Persephone is a maiden Goddess, but She is also a Goddess of growth in the sense of maturity and independence. Persephone's symbol is the pomegranate, the fruit of the Underworld. Origin: Egypt, Crete, Greece.

Rhiannon

Known also as Epona in ancient Gaul, Rhiannon is a multi-faceted deity. She is the Goddess of horses and birds, and of the sea. Nowadays, She is invoked as a Goddess of natural justice, and balance, and is a great foil for those who mistake legal probity for fairness. Rhiannon is the patron of those who are falsely accused of wrongdoing,

73

and prisoners of conscience. She builds a bridge between ideals of justice and the reality of what is really just and equitable. Rhiannon is an advocate for just causes, even if they seem to be lost causes, and a champion of those persecuted because they are different from the dominant surrounding culture. She is a refuge for those who seek asylum from persecution. Because of Her associations with travel and flight, Rhiannon is also seen as a Goddess who evinces swift change. She is also connected with moments of transition, including the passing from life into death, when the blessing amongst Goddess people is 'may the sweet birds of Rhiannon accompany your flight'. She is a mature Goddess and a protective parent. She is invoked by parents trying to protect their children, and by those who feel that they are being treated unfairly. Rhiannon's connection with the sea is really through Her role as patron of horses — the flecks of foam on breakers are known in some parts of Britain as 'mares' tails'. Rhiannon's symbols are the horse and the swallow. Origin: Wales.

Sarasvati

Goddess of learning, wisdom, music and the arts. Giver of speech and language. Her symbol is the Veena (a stringed instrument) which She holds in one of Her four arms. Her colour is yellow, and She is often depicted riding a white swan. Another symbol associated with Her is the lotus flower, representation of the soul, and of knowledge unfolding. Sarasvati brings the gifts of intuition, thought, awareness and learning. Origin: India.

Sehkmet   Lion-headed fire- and sun-Goddess. Sehkmet is seen as the destroyer of folly and excess. She has a fiery reputation, and can be invoked to help deal with unpleasant situations, such as bullying, harassment, or fearfulness. Sehkmet is a Goddess of courage and action, and has the ability to cut through our fears, and make us see situations more clearly. Her symbol is the lion, or the sun disc. She is sometimes conflated with Bast, the Egyptian cat-Goddess, and Her feline qualities are of stillness and waiting before action. She strikes down enemies swiftly and justly, and ensures that they see the error of their ways before She allows them to proceed. She is known to block those who plot against the underprivileged, and is a great favourite with those who call upon Her for empowerment. Sehkmet is a great champion of the underdog, and inspires us into action. Origin: Egypt.

Shekinah   Sometimes referred to as 'the' Shekinah, or female energy, Shekinah is also honoured as a Goddess in the Goddess spirituality movement. Shekinah is the Goddess of creative energy, which She stirs by Her dance of creation. Shekinah represents inner wisdom and the integration of hand-and-mind wisdom. She is seen in the power of intuition, and of thought. Shekinah is also manifestation, and so is seen as a facilitator, one who communicates the will. Her symbol is the feather. Origin: North Africa.

Shakti

Like Shekinah, Shakti was originally seen as the female life-force. As a Goddess, She is honoured as divine spark within, fertility of the spirit, mind and body, and the essential warmth that brings the earth to life. Shakti's symbols include the staff and drum of the wise-woman. Origin: India.

Sophia

Goddess of wisdom and spiritual love. Sophia is invoked as the inner wisdom that gives the lie to cultural and social 'truths' that bind the mind and lead to distorted thinking. Sophia, as the wisdom that resides within the heart as well as the mind, can transcend these distortions and arrive at a clear understanding. She is also the Goddess of grace — a state arrived at when we connect with, and embody the Goddess in our lives. Her symbol is the dove, or the eye. Origins: North Africa, Greece.

Selene

Selene is the Goddess of the full moon. She shines light into obscure places in order to discover hidden truths. Selene represents the true beauty that is in all of us, and reminds us that we are all differently beautiful. She is the mother aspect of the moon triad of Goddesses, and the glory and mystery of the child in the womb is seen in the shapes and shadows cast on the disc of the full moon. Selene brings to light all things in our own nature that are repressed and hidden from us. She is the light of truth, and the joy of parenthood. Selene is the Queen of High Tides of rivers and seas, and is a much-loved Goddess in the contemporary movement. Her metal is silver, and Her symbol the full moon. Origin: Greece, Italy.

Taranis

Goddess of lightning and storms, and swift justice. Taranis is invoked when we need to instigate swift action, or move and shake a situation that seems immovable. Her symbol is the wheel, which represents her ability to turn situations around dramatically. Taranis is a good Goddess to invoke in cases of abuse of authority, bullying or perjury. Origin: Britain and Northern Europe.

Vesta

Goddess of the hearth fire, and the heart of the home. Vesta presides over the well-being of families, or communities that live under one roof. She protects the sanctity of the home as a retreat and sanctuary from the outside world, a place where, ideally, we should feel safe, relaxed and valued by those who share our living space. Vesta represents the warmth of material shelter as well as the warmth of human company when friends and family gather together. She is good to invoke to keep harmony in a household, and to bring good fortune into the home. In honouring Vesta, we are actually attending to the needs of the household, and ourselves, and making sacred the space in which we are 'rooted' or have a base. Vesta's symbols are the hearth-stone, or matches. Origin: Italy.

Yemana

A sea-Goddess who rules over the mysterious and unstoppable forces of water on our planet, both in the physical sense and in terms of its spiritual meaning. The element of water represents, among other things, the emotions, love, healing and irrevocable change. Yemana is the Goddess of these facets of our existence, and is much beloved in the Santeria tradition. Her colour is blue or turquoise, and She is sometimes depicted walking out of the ocean, and covered in shells. Yemana is a Goddess of the senses and the emotions. She represents the love that exists on an everyday level, a love that is far away from the romantic ideals of novels and movies. This is the love between partners, between parents and children, and the love that binds all things in existence together. She guards the baby in the womb, and rules over dreams and prophecy. Yemana is a loving Goddess, and a powerful one to invoke in times of trouble. Her symbols are shells and turquoise. Origin: Africa, Cuba.

Exercise: Finding Your Guiding Goddess

When starting out on the path of spiritual discovery, whether alone or with friends, it is good to have a personal companion on the journey to guide and direct you on the way. The object of this exercise is to introduce you to your guiding Goddess. This is a Goddess who will remain with you throughout your early days on the path, and to whom you can turn for advice and guidance. She is a Goddess who is also *the* Goddess, and thus is also a part of you. Try to keep an open mind about who will come to you — the more fiery among you who expect a Boudicca-like figure may well be attended by a water deity, whilst gentle souls expecting a quieter aspect of the Goddess may well get a thundery storm-Goddess! Be prepared to accept whoever, and whatever comes to you. She is also part of you, so trust your own inner wisdom.

For this exercise, you will need a safe space where you will not be disturbed for about 30 minutes, your notebook and a pen.

1   *Sit or lie in a comfortable position. Relax and slow your breathing. When you are relaxed and ready to begin, close your eyes.*

2   *Concentrate on your breathing, and with each breath in, draw in strength and energy. With each breath out, breathe out stress, fatigue and anxiety. Keep exchanging wholesome energy for harmful feelings until you feel recharged.*

3   *Keeping your breathing regular, listen now to your heartbeat. It should be slow and regular after your relaxation exercise. Listen to the pulse that pumps life-giving blood around your body. It is telling you to 'Listen, listen, listen, listen ...'*

4   *Imagine you are deep beneath the ground, under a great tree, whose roots spread around to form the rafters that hold up the roof of the hollow where you are sitting. The heartbeat*

79

you are hearing comes from around, and below, as well as within you. This is the pulse of nature. Touch the ground to feel its beat, and the roots that tap into the water and minerals in the earth to nourish the living tree above you. With each beat, your heartbeat will slow to match this much larger, deeper pulse.

5   *Above you, the earth begins to crack and daylight appears. The roots are breaking through the surface soil as they grow and the pulse running through them grows stronger. The earth below you heaves upwards, and you are delivered through the crack in the earth, to the world of daylight above.*

6   *You are standing in a green forest clearing. The clearing is in the shape of a circle, and around it are oaks, hawthorns and ash trees. These are a particularly magical combination of trees, so you know that you are standing somewhere special — somewhere between the everyday world and the Otherworld. This is the threshold of the realm of Goddess Consciousness — a place that you will one day visit. Go to the centre of the space, and seat yourself on the floor.*

7   *On the ground, and to the side of you, you find a thick stick or club. Take it in both hands and bang it on the earth in front of you three times to summon your guiding Goddess.*

8   *Before you, in the clearing, a figure of a woman will appear. Take careful note of Her appearance, any symbols, totems or animals that accompany Her, and if anything happens to the clearing or the surroundings, for example, a sudden nightfall, or the appearance of particular flowers or fruit. This is your guiding Goddess.*

9   *You may ask the Goddess Her name. Do not be disheartened if She does not offer it at first — She may offer you clues instead. Make careful note of these — try not to forget in your excitement at finding your personal guardian.*

10   *Tell the Goddess that you accept Her as your guide and teacher, and wait to see if She wishes to offer you any advice.*

11   *The figure will quickly fade once She has spoken, but may leave a trace of her identity, or purpose in your life, behind Her.*

12   *When you are ready, return to the space in which you are sitting or lying. Before you eat and drink something to 'ground' yourself, quickly write down some notes on Her appearance, any symbols and any first impressions you may like to record.*

13   *If the Goddess offered Her name, and it is one that you either recognize, or find in a*

*reference book, you can research Her history,
what She represents, and learn about Her
totems and symbols. Otherwise, you may need
to research Her identity in a more roundabout
way, that brings you a different element of
understanding of Her purpose and function.
Meditate often to recall the figure, and try
to build a working relationship with Her.
You may find it helpful to have images or
representations of Her, or Her symbols around
you. If these are not readily available, consider
creating and working on some of these for
yourself.*

Notes

1   Wittig, M 1985, quoted in Harvey, 1997, page 85.

FOUR

THE GODDESS-
Centred
Cosmos

A common shape found at sites built by our ancestors is that of the spiral. It is a symbol found in various guises at Neolithic sites in Britain, Ireland and continental Europe, as well as at ancient sites around the globe. Famous examples are found at Bryn-Celi-Dubh in Wales, and Newgrange in Ireland. Archaeologists have interpreted the spiral, maze and serpentine shapes found at ancient sites as an expression of humankind's understanding of the cycles of all life. For Goddess people, the spiral represents the unending natural cycle of birth, death and regeneration — and depicts the connecting force that joins together the spokes of the great web of existence. The Goddess-centred cosmos is characterized by its sense of change and circularity — much as the spiral is a two-dimensional depiction of a circle stretched out to demonstrate how things can go around in circles, and yet change.

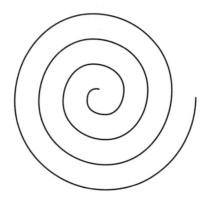

Figure 2: The spiral represents the unending natural cycle.

Understanding this way of conceptualizing the Universe means seeing things differently from the way that we have been encouraged
to within our present system of everyday 'knowledge'. One of the
ways in which to recognize this system as it stands is to consider
the meanings of time and space as they are customarily presented.
Feminist scholars and anthropologists have recently theorized that
humans have understood the concept of time very differently at various points of our development. The epoch we are now in has been
described as a time of 'Logos', the time of the rational, dividing, logical mind. During this period, humans, particularly in the west, have
understood time to be linear, and sequential. We measure time as
we conceptualize it; days, weeks, months, years ordered numerical-
ly so that we can identify them, and mark them off as they pass. We
are so far into this understanding that it is difficult to see what an
alternative view might look like. However, it is now thought that it is
highly probable that prior to the time of Logos, there was an era that
could be described as that of Mythos, the era of the 'irrational'

mind, and that this was a period in which humans understood time
as *cyclical* rather than linear. Time was measured in cycles, rather
than in straight lines, and witnessed by the processive cycles
of earth, sun, moon and stars. The symbol of the spiral makes
sense within such a way of thinking, as it represents, albeit two-
dimensionally, a process that was cyclical in nature.

The enthusiasm in the Goddess community for a more organic and
holistic understanding of life, and our place in the Universe, is not
merely based on our ancestors' penchant for spirals, however. We
neither are, nor wish to be, carbon copies of a long-dead culture.
Taking our inspiration from ancient symbols, and imagining what
these may have meant to people in Neolithic times, is only one part
of the story. Our current concepts and symbols of cyclic reality are

also based on the discoveries of our own era. Recent advances in technology have enabled us to discover that both the largest, and smallest, formations in our Universe are characterized by spirals. Both the microcosmic double helix of DNA, the blueprint of life, and, at the other extreme, our own galaxy, the Milky Way, are spiral in shape. Just as DNA holds the secret of life, so the nebulae within spiralling galaxies are the birthplace of stars. The spiral, then, is quite literally revealed as a primordial shape that describes the process of constant renewal at microcosmic and macrocosmic levels.

Current scientific understanding of the time-space continuum can also be reflected by the symbol of the spiral. The vast distances involved in measuring the known Universe force us to speak in terms of time, as well as distance, and calculations of the age of stars, galaxies and the Universe are made by their distance from us. This very modern concept of the relationship between time and space, and the multi-dimensional nature of reality, is captured, oddly enough, in the symbols left by our ancestors on sacred sites, millennia before the amazing discoveries made within the last generation. Perhaps our ancestors, in a relationship with nature which was very different from our own, intuited correctly from the deep pulse of the cycles they measured by, the essential cyclical nature of all existence.

The Cosmos of those who are Goddess-centred, then, is a series of interconnecting cycles. We see all life as processive, rather than linear, in its nature. For us, there are no precise beginnings and endings, and for us nothing in the Universe truly ends. All things in the Universe change, and when destroyed in one form, provide the material for the growth of another — for us this is a spiritual truth, as well as a fact of physics. Death itself is seen as a process that produces material changes, and although opinions on the exact format of this process differ, it is generally agreed that we are spiritually and physically 'recycled'. Just as, at the cosmic level, matter is reformed, even at the death and birth of stars, so we see our lives as one part of a process in which we act upon and affect all around us, then go on to form something else when our individual consciousness ceases at physical death.

Understanding this concept of being — or more accurately, becoming — means entering what is referred to as Goddess-consciousness. This is a time-space in which the concepts of Mythos and Logos are both combined and made different. Here, thought and logic are altered by their contact with the world of intuition, creativity and myth-making. To enter Goddess-consciousness, or the Space-between-the-worlds, is to discover the endless potential of creativity within, and between, humans: it is the spiritual equivalent of the nebulae within spiral galaxies, out of which stars are formed.

The interplay between Mythos and Logos enables us to enter an enchanted, magical realm in which we encounter the Goddess. She waits for us in a place that is accessed via symbols, but is not ruled by them. We approach Her by allowing our intuitive and thinking selves to merge, and by trusting ourselves to interpret Her symbols, without demanding that they be pinned down, defined and catalogued. The way into the magical realm of Goddess-consciousness is both a tiny step and a huge leap. It requires what may appear to be a great deal of us, but will, in retrospect, seem very little — putting aside the world of straight lines, boxes and conventional 'knowledge' from time to time, in order to discover and recreate our conception of reality.

In order to edge towards entering this type of consciousness, it is necessary to acknowledge the cycles of life around us. In Goddess spirituality, we celebrate those cycles with which we are most intimately involved. Those we experience collectively are the cycles of our own planet in relation to its parent, the Sun, and its companion, the Moon.

Cycles of Sun and Earth

The harmonious rhythms of Sun, Moon and Earth engender a series of markers, or points within cycles, which we can celebrate. The lengthiest of these cycles is that of the dance between the Sun and the Earth. Because of the tilt of the Earth's axis, we experience different seasons. In Britain, the USA and Europe, where contemporary Goddess spirituality first evolved, these different seasons have a number of traditional festivals attached. Some of these festivals, known as the 'solar festivals', are astronomical events with definitive dates attached. Others, known as 'fire festivals', because of their reputed links with the ancient Celts and their habit of lighting fires at times of celebration, are not as fixed, and tend to wait upon signs of the changing seasons, such as crop harvests, or changes in the weather.

There are four solar festivals, which divide the Earth-Sun year into exact quarters. The winter solstice (solstice comes from the Latin for Sun and stillness), when the time of daylight is shortest, celebrates both the shortest day, and the 'return' of the sun and the lengthening of days thereafter. This is the festival of Yule, which falls on 21 or 22 December. At the Spring Equinox, when the length of light and darkness in a twenty-four hour period is exactly equal and balanced, we celebrate the festival of Eostre, or Ostara. This falls on 21 or 22 March, whereafter the hours of daylight are greater than the hours of darkness in the course of one day. At the summer solstice, or 'longest day', we celebrate Litha (meaning 'wheel'), the triumph of light. From this date, 21 or 22 July, although the best of summer is generally yet to come, the hours of daylight actually diminish again. On 21 or 22 September, at the Autumnal Equinox, or Modron, daylight and darkness are again of equal length, though this time the hours of daylight diminish up until the Winter Solstice.

Set between these astronomical markers of the dance between the Sun and the Earth are the fire festivals. Around the beginning of February, when snowdrops appear as the harbingers of Spring, and the snow and ice of winter melt, the festival of Imbolc is set. Meaning 'ewes' milk', it coincides with the season of lambing in farming communities, and the mating and birthing of animals in the wild. This festival is predominantly a woman's festival, and is dedicated to Brighid, the Goddess of fire, healing and crafts.

The next fire festival is celebrated on or around 1 May and is known as Beltane. This is a festival of early summer, and celebrates the greening and fertility of the earth. It is a time of 'Faery' — when the veil between the worlds is thin, and mischief and fun are afoot. Beltane (meaning 'fires of Bel') celebrates fertility, commitment and raucous sexuality!

The fire festival celebrated around the end of July and the beginning of August — the time of the cereal harvest — is Lughnasadh. It is a time when we commemorate the cutting down of the corn for the good of the people, and celebrate the harvest. The mysteries of life, death and regeneration are seen in the cereal cycle, and this festival sees many of us renewing our commitment to ensuring that this cycle is not damaged by changes in climate, pollution, or technological interference with the crop itself.

The fire festival between the Autumnal Equinox and the Winter Solstice comes in the midst of what we call the Dark Season, and is called 'Samhain', meaning 'first frosts'. Celebrated at the end of October, and otherwise known as 'Hallowe'en', Samhain is the festival of the Dead, of the Ancestors.

This procession of eight festivals — Yule, Imbolc, Eostre, Beltane, Litha, Lughnasadh, Modron and Samhain, provides points at which we can mark the processes of our existence. Importantly, they provide an opportunity for making connections between the physical changes around us with the spiritual changes within. Just as the physical harvest of Lughnasadh is a time for pondering the wonders of the cycle of birth, death and regeneration, it can also be a time to celebrate the fruits of our labours, and blessings that have come to us since the last harvest. Samhain, Day of the Dead, marks the death of the summer's greenery, and commemorates people who have died. At the same time, it is also a period for remembering things in our life that have come to an end, and honouring them appropriately. The eight festivals of the Goddess year, then, represent cycles at a personal, experiential, and literal, physical level.

Exercise: Goddess of the Seasons

The purpose of this exercise is to help you assimilate the idea of the cycle of the year and become familiar with the Goddesses and inner and outer cycles associated with them. Read through Section A and, using your notebook, write down your answers to the questions set under the description of each festival. Section B contains a list of possible answers to compare with your own. You may wish to cover Section B with a sheet of paper so that you are not distracted.

Section A

1 Yule — the Winter Solstice

Set on 21/22 December, on the shortest day, Yule celebrates 'sun-return' as the days lengthen thereafter. Yule signals the birth of the sun-child, and sees the Goddess both giving birth, and being born. Some of the most popular associations of the festival are: evergreens, especially holly and ivy, mistletoe; candlelight; star symbols, which of course represent the sun; glittery items to catch and reflect light, and the joy of community with others. With all this in mind, consider the following;

a) *Which Goddess, or Goddess aspect, might it be appropriate to celebrate at this time of year?*

b) *Why are evergreens an important symbol at this particular festival, and what do you think they represent?*

c) *Which aspects or events in your personal life might it be appropriate to celebrate, or honour at Yule?*

2 Imbolc

Known in the Christian church as 'Candlemas', Imbolc marks the fact that winter is loosening its grip on the earth, and the days are noticeably lengthening. It is the time of early thaw, and some of the first shoots are pushing through. Many cereal crops are sown at this time, if the soil is thawed enough. Imbolc is predominantly a women's festival, and sometimes has the atmosphere of a confinement. In some circles, an old tradition is re-enacted — the making of the 'Bridiog'. This is a straw, or other, effigy of the Goddess

Brighid, either as a woman or as a baby, which is placed in a basket, and clothed and decorated by the women. Secrets and wishes are whispered to Her in the course of the celebrations, and she is treated like a real person. Brighid, and Imbolc, are strongly associated with serpents, and mounds. See if you can answer the following questions:

a) *Why is it, do you think, that Brighid is a Goddess of the early thaw?*

b) *Is Imbolc a good time to:*

   i) *make promises?*
   ii) *cast spells for new projects?, or*
   iii) *get rid of old habits, or feelings?*

c) *Why is it, do you think, that grown women make/place a doll in a basket to celebrate this festival?*

3 Eostre — the Spring or Vernal Equinox

The festival of Eostre is set at the Spring Equinox, when day and night are of equal length, and the hours of daylight lengthen thereafter. Most closely associated with the Goddess Eostre, it is a time of balance, and celebrates the fertility of the earth with symbols such as the egg and the hare. This festival occurs nine months before the rebirth of the sun at Yule, and so is closely connected with conception, as well as the birth of greenery and young animals that take place at this time of year. Consider these questions:

a)   *Which Goddesses or Goddess aspects, besides Eostre, might be celebrated at this time?*

b)   *What aspect of your personal life might it be appropriate to celebrate at Eostre?*

c)   *Why is the hare seen as a fertility symbol, do you think?*

4 Beltane

Beltane takes place around 1 May, or when the May tree is in bloom. Day is now noticeably longer than night, and it grows warmer. It is customary to eat and give nuts as gifts and favours at this festival, and wear foliage masks in honour of the green wo/man, a spirit of nature and vegetation. Maypoles with ribbons and circlets of flowers decorate village greens and ritual space at this feast. Beltane marks the beginning of summer, the lush greenery around us, and the manifestation of earth's fertility. Beltane is both a time of sexual licence and for making commitments. Consider the following:

a)   *Which Goddesses might be honoured at Beltane?*

b)   *What personal and/or community events might appropriately take place at Beltane?*

c)   *What aspect of your personal life might it be appropriate to celebrate at Beltane?*

5 Litha — the Summer Solstice

Litha is celebrated on the actual date of the solstice — 21/22 June — and marks the longest day. This is the time when the sun is at the height of its powers, and when the days following will begin, imperceptibly at first, to shorten immediately after. Litha is the time for gathering energy to take us through the rest of the summer. It is a festival that usually involves an all-night vigil to welcome the sun as it rises on the Longest Day. People in the British Isles still gather together at stone circles, Iron Age forts, important Neolithic burial sites and hill-tops to celebrate together. Try to answer the following:

a) *Which Goddesses, or aspects of the Goddess, might it be appropriate to honour at this time of year?*

b) *What do you think is the significance of groups keeping vigil together all night to greet the Sun on the Longest Day?*

c) *Which personal aspects of your life might you focus upon at Litha?*

6 Lughnasadh

Lughnasadh, the harvest festival, takes place at the beginning of August, or at the harvest of the corn crop. It is both a celebration of plenty, and a reminder of the mystery of life, death and regeneration. We celebrate, and are grateful for the gift of harvest, and are mindful of the labour that created the crop, and of the sacrifice involved in the cutting down of the corn. One of the symbols of the harvest is the poppy, sometimes called 'Blood on the Corn'. At this time of year, corn dollies are created to house the spirit of the corn so that it will return the following year. Consider the following:

> a)   *Which Goddesses or aspects of the Goddess might it be appropriate to honour at this time of year?*
>
> b)   *What other symbols, besides the poppy, might be associated with this festival?*
>
> c)   *What aspect of your personal and inner life is represented at this festival, do you think?*

7 Modron — the Autumnal Equinox

Modron celebrates the fruit harvest, and the balance of darkness and light. After this equinox, there are more hours of darkness than light. Nature's gifts are most manifest at this time, both in cultivated crops and in the wild. In the circle of the year, Modron is situated in the 'west' of the circle — the place of the sunset. Our ancestors thought that this was where souls went to after death — a land of eternal summer. Those who lived near the great western ocean — the Atlantic — referred to the spirits of the dead traversing the water to go to the Isle of the Blessed, Land of Eternal Youth, or Tir-nan-Og. In Arthurian legend, the dying King is transported towards the west by nine maidens (the Triple-Triple Goddess). This is a time of water, of departing summer, as well as enjoying the goodies that nature, and our labour, has provided for us. The fruit symbols of Modron are the apple and the pomegranate. Try to answer the following:

> a)   *What does this festival have in common with Lughnasadh?*
>
> b)   *Does this festival bring to mind any Goddess/es or myths that have been mentioned in this book so far?*

c)   *Do you know any stories about apples that might be linked with this festival?*

8 Samhain

Also known as Hallowe'en in Christian circles, Samhain is the Day of the Dead, and the Feast of Ancestors. Samhain means 'first frosts' and it is likely that, in prehistoric times, beasts were slaughtered at this point, before winter began in earnest, thus associating it with blood and death. Samhain is popularly associated with witches, bats, monsters, spiders, darkness and ghosts. Goddess people put some of these symbols to positive use in order to celebrate death as a part of life, to honour those who have gone before us into death, and to value the concept of 'darkness'. Try if you can to answer the following:

a)   *Which Goddess/es or Goddess aspect might it be appropriate to honour at Samhain?*

b)   *What might be valuable about the concept of darkness that is honoured at this festival?*

c)   *What positive personal and/or political aspects of your life might be celebrated at Samhain?*

Section B — Suggested Answers

The answers below should be considered merely as suggestions and prompts. Since many of the questions asked what you *thought*, and because spirituality is such a personal journey, none of the suggested answers should be considered in any way definitive. Compare them with your own and see if you change your mind, or feel compelled to explain further why you have chosen the answers you have jotted down. Take the time to scribble a few further notes to yourself, and return to them again as you work your way through the book.

1   *Yule*

a)   *Any sun-Goddess, the crone in her midwife aspect, or any mother-Goddess. Nemesis, who sometimes represents the long dark night of the soul, is an ideal Goddess to represent the darkness of the season, but Her presence could be balanced with a Sun-deity, such as Bel, or Sol.*

b)   *Evergreens represent the eternal nature of life, and symbolize the faithful promise of the Goddess of the land to send us greenery the next year. They are important at this festival because they grow even when the earth is at its darkest, and in the grip of winter.*

c)   *You might consider celebrating the inner spark that re-energizes us even when things seem at their darkest. Even when life seems quiet on the surface, seeds of ideas are germinating beneath the soil.*

2   *Imbolc*

a)   *Brighid is a sun and fire goddess, and an ideal symbol of the warming up of the earth.*

b)   i)   *Not really — Beltane would be better for this. You could, however, use Imbolc as a time to 'plant the seeds' of your commitment to projects — especially those involving justice for women, children and animals.*

    ii)   *You could, yes. It is also a good time for 'scrying' into the future year.*

    iii)   *This is really best done at Samhain, the time of death and 'shedding', at Lughnasadh, where the 'chaff' is separated from the wheat, or as part of your 'Spring cleaning' at Eostre. However, Imbolc is a time of renewal, so it is a good time for putting aside old grudges or hatreds, for example, and renewing relationships.*

c)   *This element of playfulness is really to reflect the idea of 'innocence' and renewal that goes with the festival. It gives adults, who are, in some cultures, forced to 'grow up' too quickly, a chance to play and make things that many of us haven't experienced since early childhood. Goddess spirituality values this form of creativity, and since the Bridiog is a genuinely-kept tradition in rural communities in parts of Celtic Britain, it seems fitting for this particular festival.*

3   *Eostre*

a)   *Any Spring deities — for example Maia or
      Persephone. Some Earth Goddesses, such as
      Andraste, whose symbol is the hare, are also
      appropriate.*

b)   *It is usually considered a good time to
      celebrate literal fertility — pregnancy,
      lactation, birth or parenthood — and
      metaphorical fertility, such as your creative
      talents, or other potentials.*

c)   *The hare, called in Scotland the 'cat o' the
      fields', is seen cavorting and boxing with
      others at this time of year in a mating dance.
      Rabbits and hares are sometimes conflated at
      this festival, as both are notoriously fast-
      breeding animals.*

4   *Beltane*

a)   *The most obvious is Bel, for whom the festival
      is named. Otherwise, any Goddess who
      signifies fertility. The Goddess as Queen of the
      May is an appropriate aspect, as are Astarte
      and Aphrodite, Goddesses of love and physical
      passion.*

b)   *Beltane has long been associated with workers
      and labour, so political events take place at
      this time of year. This makes it a good time to*

*express your commitment to life-affirming,
political causes. It is also a good time for
'handfasting' or getting married. Many
couples make promises to each other and
jump over the broomstick to seal the deal at
Beltane.*

c)   *It is a good time for making promises and
pledges, particularly those involved with
overcoming difficulties in your life, or
promoting health.*

5   *Litha*

a)   *Sun- and Fire-Goddesses, especially Bel or
Amaterasu. Goddesses of poetry, inspiration,
courage or the will are also appropriate. Kali,
a fire Goddess who encapsulates the life force,
is a good Goddess to honour at this time.*

b)   *Being together at this time through the short
hours of darkness encourages a camaraderie
that, at all night vigils in the open, warms the
inner sun in all of us. Telling stories and
singing songs by the fires that are often lit
during this night strengthens the sister/
brotherhood of the fireside and reminds us of
the light that we can bring to each other in
darkness, on the festival of the power of the
sun.*

c)   *You might concentrate on empowering*
      yourself and others, renewing your
      energies, and attending to your health — all
      associations of the sun.

6   *Lughnasadh*

a)   *Demeter, or Ceres, and Habundia, all*
      Goddesses of the Harvest. It is also good to be
      mindful of the Crone Goddess, whose scythe
      cuts down the corn.

b)   *A sheaf of corn or a loaf of bread would be*
      good symbols of this harvest. Otherwise, in
      places where the squash harvest comes early,
      various squashes.

c)   *The aspect of our ability to let go of things*
      that do us more good if they are cut away.
      This is a good time for separating out what is,
      and isn't useful in our lives. It is also a great
      time for celebrating the blessings that have
      come to us in the last year, and for sharing
      those blessings with others. This might entail
      renewing our commitment to ensuring that
      all peoples are as fortunate, and that the
      harvest is uncontaminated by pollution or
      technological interference.

7   *Modron*

a)   Like Lughnasadh, Modron celebrates the
     gathering in of fruitfulness. And like
     Lughnasadh, Modron also involves endings.

b)   The Goddesses and myth most popularly
     associated with this festival make up
     the Demeter-Persephone myth, and the
     pomegranate seeds that Persephone ate whilst
     in the realm of the dead are commemorated
     by the symbol of the pomegranate — the fruit
     of wisdom.

c)   The apple is another fruit of wisdom. The
     Jewish myth of Adam and Eve might spring
     to mind — this signalled the beginning of
     wisdom, but the end of innocence/ignorance.
     It was also a time of leaving — in this
     case the legendary Garden of Eden. Those
     interested in the Arthurian cycle link the
     festival to the passing of summer into the
     west — to Avalon, the Isle of Apples.

8.   Samhain

a)   This is the season of the Crone and the Hag.
     The Calliach (Old Woman), Ceridwen of the
     cauldron, or Hecate are appropriate Goddesses
     to honour at Samhain — also Persephone in
     her aspect as Queen of the Dead.

b)   It might be considered to be a way of
     confronting our fears of the dark, of things

that we find monstrous, and of the fear of
death. Some parents actually use this festival
as a way of allowing children free reign with
their imaginations, in order to let them come
to terms with their imaginary 'monsters'.

c)   Personal aspects might include remembering
our own beloved dead, coming to terms with
our own mortality and allowing ourselves a
real occasion to grieve for, and talk with,
the dead. Political aspects might include
honouring the dead of wars, injustice and
discrimination. Some groups hold open
or public rituals at this time for this very
purpose.

Exercise: Keeping the Festivals

The aim of this exercise is to build upon the knowledge you have
already gained about the festivals and the cycle of the year, by
beginning to draw up a personal list of associations with the various
festivals.

1   In your notebook, draw a table with nine rows
and six columns. On the first row of the first
column, write the word 'Festival', and list in
the eight rows beneath, beginning with Yule,
the names and dates of the eight festivals.

2   Along the top of the table, in the five
remaining columns in the first row, write

these words: 'Goddess'; 'Symbols'; 'Cycle of
Nature'; 'Inner meaning'; 'Activities'. You
should now have a table with the eight festival
names written in the far left-hand column,
and five aspects of the festivals written in the
first row, along the top.

3   Spend some time re-reading the descriptions
and purposes of the festivals before
proceeding further, and check back for details
when you need to.

4   Over the period of about a week, work your
way through the festivals and try to decide
which Goddesses, symbols, cycle in nature,
inner meaning and activities are most
appropriate to each of them. Begin with what
you already know from reading this book. You
can also check in some of the other books I
have listed in the recommended reading section
to find inspiration for other associations. You
should also meditate on the festivals, and think
about the rhythm and cycle of your year, and
how the Goddess year fits with it.

5   When you have ideas for Goddesses, symbols,
etc, write them down in the table you have
prepared. You may find, in time, as you
become more expert and adept at intuiting
symbols and associations, that the number of
columns grows, and the associations listed
within them expand.

6   *When you have finished making your table,*
albeit one with spaces for further additions as
and when inspiration strikes, try to work
out where you are in relation to the cycle of
festivals right now. Which is the next one?

7   *Hopefully, you will be feeling inspired to test*
out some of your new-found knowledge about
the cycles of the Sun, and celebrate the next
festival. When you have read chapters seven
and nine, you will have enough knowledge to
be able to construct your own Goddess rituals,
and allow your imagination to run wild in
finding ways of celebrating the passage of the
year!

Cycles of the Moon

The path of the moon around the Earth, and the different phases created by the Sun's light upon the Moon's surface, give us the different phases of the Moon. The word 'month' means literally 'moon-th', or cycle of the moon. Although most calendar months are 30—31 days, the actual time taken for the moon to go from New, or Dark Moon, through crescent, quarter (half), full, quarter, crescent and back to Dark again, is 29.5 days. One solar year actually contains almost twelve and a half moon cycles, so that in each solar year there is at least one moon phase (Dark/first quarter, full, last quarter) that is repeated not twelve, but thirteen times. This leads to the assertion, among Goddess people and other moon-wise folk, that there are actually thirteen moons in a year. Women who menstruate regularly will tend to have thirteen, rather than twelve periods of bleeding in the course of one year, so we consider the notion of thirteen moons, rather than twelve calendar 'months' to be more natural. Goddess people tend to disregard the numbers and days of calendar months, and refer instead to 'moons', meaning 'one moon cycle'.

In Goddess spirituality, as in many spiritual and magical traditions, like Witchcraft and Paganism, the phases of the moon have an inner, personal, psychological significance as well as an outer, physical and magical one. For us, the Moon, which reflects the light of the Sun, is also a Mirror of the Soul, which shows us our true selves. The Moon's gravitational pull affects tidal seas and rivers, as well as the habits of plants and animals. At a psychological level, many of us notice that our dreams change with the Moon's phases, as do our emotional energies. The powers of the Moon have always been tinged with an air of mystery, or even fear: it was believed, even in the last century, that spending too long in the moonlight could encourage madness or derangement. Nowadays, Witches, Pagans and Goddess people celebrate beneath the Moon as a way of recognizing its amazing effects on life on earth.

The Moon traditionally presides over the realm of dreams. Although the purpose and nature of dreams is still not properly understood by scientists, it is recognized that some of our dreams reveal a great deal to us about ourselves, and what is happening in our lives. Dreaming remains, for the large part, one of the most mysterious aspects of our existence, which in turn can be one of the most revelatory. In Goddess spirituality, we try to understand our dreams as mediators between our inner and outer lives, and our emotional and logical selves. Just as the Moon reflects the light of the Sun back to Earth, our dreams reflect back to us the truth about ourselves — our own 'inner Suns'. The Moon is an ambiguous symbol, representing both that which is hidden, and that which is revealed. Psychologically, magically and spiritually, it functions as both mask and mirror.

Dreams, like the Moon, also have a magical and spiritual dimension. They are the part of us that has always entered Goddess consciousness — the space between the worlds. Our dreams are a corridor, along which symbols are sent as clues to messages sent from self to self. Goddess people, who consider the Goddess as connection, consider these clues as also coming from the Goddess. These clues can appear as puns, or as magical symbols. Some years ago, a friend had a strange dream in which she was chasing chickens. She ran up and down the road, warning the neighbours that the chickens had escaped, until she was tired, and had to give up. As a town-dweller, she was unfamiliar with the habits of live chickens, and could not understand why she had dreamed something so odd. When she discussed this dream with her friends from the Goddess circle she was attending, she was encouraged to think about it in terms of a linguistic pun. She pretty quickly realized it meant that she was 'chickening out' of something, and immediately identified the situation. She had been getting rather worn down by a friend who was constantly complaining, rather unreasonably, about the behaviour of a mutual friend of theirs. Due to her interpreting the dream in this way, she could resolve the situation by talking things through with her, and persuading her to consider whether her complaints were fair. In this case, the wise-woman within had sent a message to be interpreted by her waking self, in order to warn her that her inaction was threatening her own well-being, and she was able to act on it.

Some dreams bear symbols that are not quite as obvious. Deciphering these can be part of the journey towards spiritual understanding. A friend was bothered for many years by a recurring dream in which she entered a haunted house, only to be pursued by a skeleton, which she felt to be threatening and malevolent. When she started to explore her own spirituality, and open up her intuitive powers, the dreams began to change, and become more terrifying, as the skeleton got closer and closer to catching her each time the dream occurred. She decided to see what would happen if she allowed the skeleton to catch her, so the next time she had this dream, during the chase, she became aware that it *was* a dream and slowed down to face the skeleton figure. To her surprise, the skeleton stepped forward into her body and merged with her, and she awoke feeling peaceful and happy. She never dreamed that particular dream again. Months after this breakthrough, she came across a reference to skeletons in Clarissa Pinkola Estes' *Women Who Run With The Wolves* (1989). In this book, an old woman sang back to life the bones of animals. My friend realized that the haunted house was a reference to her own state of mind — that she had been literally 'haunted' by an event from 30 years earlier when she had been abused by a neighbour. The skeleton was, on one level, a 'skeleton in the closet', but as the symbols of the bones in the book pointed out to her — those were *her* bones, *her* peace of mind, which she could reclaim and take into herself. Her powers became, like those of the old woman in the desert, creative and magical. In order to sing her own bones into life, she had first to claim them back.

The Moon sings over our bones, too, in a way. The Old Woman of the Moon calls out to us and encourages us to *become* — to open ourselves up to Her mysteries and reflections and strip away all pretension, all the restraints of convention. Not all of what we have been taught throughout our lives is true, and the Moon is an empowering symbol for those who seek beneath lies and other forms of illusion. When Goddess people dance beneath the Moon, we do not become mad, but free from some of the madness we find around us. We use the cycle of the moon to keep in touch with our intuitive, magical powers, and our emotional, knowing selves. In Goddess spirituality, the changes of the moon represent the changes in our lives, and the eternal cycle of all existence. Attuning ourselves to its rhythms is a constant reminder of the physical and spiritual reality of change, and a way of beginning to link with the energies of nature that we find around us. Just as the moon's gravitational pull creates tides in the oceans, so it creates a psychological and psychic effect on humans. Since we are all different, we have to find out for ourselves what this close interconnection of human-lunar rhythms means to us as individuals, and, if you are going to be working with a group at some time in the future, as communities.

Exercise: Keeping a moon diary

This exercise aims to help you gauge the effect that the moon has on your physical, emotional and psychic energies, and your dreams. You will need to make enough space in the back of your notebook to record these cycles over three moons. You are also advised to start keeping a separate dream diary, which should be kept with a pen by your bed, so that you can record shorthand details of dreams if you wake up in the night.

1 *Over the course of three months, keep notes in your notebook of the phase of the moon (i.e. one day after Dark Moon, two days after, etc), and jot down how you feel first thing in the morning, and last thing at night. Note any emotional changes, as well as physical changes — women especially are asked to note down which period of the moon coincides with their menstrual bleeding.*

2 Use the dream diary in a similar way, only keep it by your bed, as a word or two written down about a dream you have woken from in the night can help you to remember your dreams more easily — it is amazing how much we forget! Write in the date and the moon-phase, so that you can look back to see if there are any patterns in your dreaming life and the lunar cycle.

3 Spend some time out of doors looking at the moon — what pictures can you see in the face of the Moon? Is is a woman, a hare, a baby in the womb? What does its shadows signify for you? Jot down your thoughts in the notebook.

4 Light a candle at full moon to celebrate Selene, the Goddess in her aspect of full-blooded womanhood and beauty. Try sitting a while with the lit candle, thinking what Selene represents to you. Note down any thoughts or impressions that come to you when you have finished meditating on this.

5 Try doing the same at different phases of the Moon — invoking Artemis at the waxing crescent Hunter's Moon, Hecate at the waning crescent Sickle Moon, and Lilith at Dark Moon. Note down everything that comes to you, as these notes are handy to refer to later when you are planning full rituals or celebrations of the lunar cycle.

6   *Find out as much as you can about
superstitions, traditions and spells to do with
the Moon, and see whether any of these match
your understanding of the lunar cycle. Note
down anything interesting that you find
and compare it with your own thoughts or
feelings about the Moon.*

Goddess of the Elements

Goddess people consider that all life is made up of five elements — Air, Fire, Water, Earth and Spirit. Each of these elements represents different aspects of existence, and all have associated symbols and meanings attached to them. We use the symbols of the elements to artificially separate out what in nature is naturally interlinking and overlapping. We do this to simplify the way that we represent certain things in magical spells, rituals and ceremonies, where it is always best to keep things simple. We also use symbols of and references to elements in order to empower ourselves, as you will see. Taking the symbols one by one, then, these are their different meanings, symbols and associations.

Air

From our first breath in this world, we use air to burn the energy that helps our bodies function. The air of our planet is essential to our survival and that of plants and animals. Because of the association between air and birds in flight, air has come to represent communication and travel. Perhaps also because birds can see things from a different angle, air also represents clarity and incisive thinking. The symbol for air is an upward-pointing equilateral triangle, traversed halfway through by a horizontal line. The equilateral triangle (upwards pointing) is also a symbol of Athena, Goddess of wisdom and learning. Other Goddesses of learning and communication are associated with this element. The magical colour given for air in many traditions is yellow — the colour of the sunrise, and the direction associated with air is East.

Fire

The parent of our planet is the sun, and it can be argued that the Earth was originally created because of the fires and energies in the Universe that created the galaxies and stars. The Sun, the key source of energy, light and heat on Earth, represents fire in its most natural aspect. Fire is energy; it is the pulse that leaps from synapse to synapse, and the spark of all life. Because we associate heat with action, and sometimes even anger, fire has come to represent courage and the will. Because light is also associated with seeing clearly, fire is also associated with inspiration and creativity — especially in poetry and the arts. The symbol for fire is a plain upwards-pointing equilateral triangle. Kali, whose wild dance is the catalyst for the creative moment, is closely associated with the element of fire. Other Goddesses of courage, empowerment, and light are also associated with Fire. The magical colour given for fire in many traditions is red — symbolizing the heat of the sun at noon, and the direction associated with fire is South.

Water

We float, dreaming and growing in water before birth, and 80 per cent of our bodies is H_2O-based. The first creatures to breathe air, and evolve into animals and humans, came from the oceans, and so water is associated with birth, irrevocable change, and dreams. Because of the contradictions bound up in the physical behaviour of water — it always finds its balance, and it can also be unsettled, turbulent — water is also associated with the emotions, and the balance of healing. The emotion to which this element is most related in magical terms, is that of love. The symbol for water is a downwards-pointing equilateral triangle — the shape of the womb. Aphrodite, Goddess of love, is often depicted rising from the ocean on a scallop shell, and is closely associated with the element of water. Other Goddesses of love and healing are also associated with water. The magical colour given for water in many traditions is blue — a symbol reflected in map-making, and the direction associated with water is West, the direction of sunset.

Earth

Earth is matter, from which we, and the planet are made. The earth, and we, are made of what has been referred to as 'star-stuff' — material arising out of the natural cycles of the universe. We build our shelters and houses out of materials gleaned from the earth, and our food is grown in its rich soil and minerals. All wealth — and by this is meant the positive essentials of life, rather than purely fiscal evaluation — comes from the earth, which is the treasure house of our existence. Earth represents stability, fertility, growth and manifestation. In magic, we refer to the element of earth when we are working towards material growth and material creation. The symbol for earth is the downwards-pointing equilateral triangle traversed halfway through with a horizontal line. Demeter, Goddess of the fertile earth, and bringer of crops, is closely associated with the element of earth. Other Goddesses of growth and fertility are also associated with it. The magical colour for earth in many traditions is green, and it is associated with the sun at midnight, which sinks below the horizon, and the direction associated with earth is North.

Spirit

Spirit is the element of connection, and is present where the other elements combine to produce life and interaction. The fact that

Spirit does not have a separate, physical presence outside of its formative, connective function does not make it any less real; quite the contrary. It is a crucial connecting force that gives form to the products of the other elements. Spirit represents interconnection and interdependence, at many different levels. It is the element of transformation, and magic. Its symbol is the web, or the spiral. Grandmother Spider, Goddess of connection, transformation, wisdom and change, is closely associated with the element of Spirit. Other Goddesses of magic and weaving are also associated with this element. The magical colour for Spirit in many traditions is purple, and the direction most associated with Spirit is at the centre of the other elements.

The Elements Together

Many Goddess women see the elements in the form of an upward-pointing, and interlinking, five pointed star. The element of spirit is represented at its apex, whilst air is at its right-hand upper point, fire at its right-hand lower point, earth at its left-hand lower point and water at its left-hand upper point. This is also the symbol of the witches — which some of us also are. This symbol is very dear to us as it represents the interlinking of all of the elements of life. To emphasize the holism of this sacred symbol, known as a pentacle, it is sometimes seen encircled, as a pentagram.

Exercise: Getting to Grips With the Elements

This exercise will help you to build an understanding of the various associations of the five elements. Use your notebook — and your imagination!

1   Turn a page in your notebook into a table
     with six rows and five columns.

2   *In the left-hand column, in the first row, write the word 'Element', and list below it in the same column, but on different rows, the names of the five elements: Air; Fire; Water; Earth; Spirit.*

3   *On the first row, and at the head of each column, write one of the following words; 'Goddess'; 'Symbols'; 'Inner meaning'; 'Activities'.*

4   *Below each of these headings, and on the appropriate row, note down details that you have read about in this chapter.*

5   *When you have done this, start to think about some alternative symbols, Goddesses, inner meanings and activities with which the different elements might be associated — for example, you may feel that Hathor or Rhiannon are excellent Goddesses of the elements of water, or a feather or bird a great alternative symbol for air.*

6   *Keep returning to your table whenever you are inspired to note down something new, as this will make a great source of notes for planning your own magical spells, ceremonies and rituals in the future.*

Now that you have been introduced to different facets of the Goddess-centred Cosmos, through the cycles of the Earth, Sun and Moon, and the elements, you may wish to get some hands-on experience of some of the concepts. You can do this in a number of ways — some have already been suggested — but what is important is that whatever you do to honour and celebrate the mysteries of the living Universe, it must make sense and have meaning to *you*. This book is intended to give you a framework around which to weave your own web — after all, Goddess spirituality is a living, changing pathway, not one set down in stone or in instruction manuals. Living in a Goddess-centred cosmos may take a little practice, but once you become attuned to the rhythms of life and change around you, you will realize that it actually is the most natural thing in the world.

FIVE

THE GODDESS
Within

The Goddess can be experienced in the cycles of nature, the patterns found in the most microcosmic element of life, and the largest structures in the Universe. But the Goddess can also be experienced *within*. In the last chapter, mention was made of a 'wise woman within', with reference to innate, inner wisdom. In Goddess spirituality, that wisdom is personified as an aspect of the Goddess — the Old Wise Woman, the self that gives us signals when all is not well, and upon whom we can draw when we are not sure what the truth is, in difficult or confusing situations. The concept of the Goddess within is a familiar one in most Goddess-centred traditions. The beautiful speech known as 'Charge of the Goddess', made in some Goddess-circles at full-moon celebrations, reminds us that:

> *If that which you seek, is not found within you,*
> *you will never find it without you. For I have*
> *been with you from the beginning ...*

It is important to us that we find the Goddess within, if we are to find Her anywhere else. Without discovering Her inside of us, we cannot progress any further down a spiritual path that honours connections. In this case, we need to make a connection between the way that we experience the Goddess around us, and the way that we experience Her within ourselves.

This sense of 'Goddess-within' is particularly important in Goddess spirituality. For women, it is particularly empowering to know that, in spite of the tales that self-appointed experts have told about women for centuries, we have an inner knowledge, and self-authority that tells us differently. For men, the idea of wisdom and authority residing within a person offers an alternative form of authority to that offered them within patriarchal cultures. The way that the Goddess community describes this idea, taking our lead from Starhawk, a well-known proponent of Goddess spirituality in the US, is as 'power-within'. This is entirely different from having power *over*, as it leads us to *em*-power rather than *disem*-power others.

There are many ways of getting to know the Goddess within, and this chapter will offer a variety of exercises and ways of discovering Her.

The Goddess as Aspects of Self

One of the ways in which Goddess is encountered within us is as different aspects of ourselves. In chapter two, you were invited to identify which aspects of the triple Goddess you could relate to in terms of where you are in your life. In so doing, you have already begun to consider different aspects of the Goddess that match with different aspects of yourself. Now that you know a little more about different Goddesses, however, you may find that specific Goddesses best describe various aspects of yourself.

Once you begin working with different Goddesses, in rituals, spells and visualizations, you will find it much easier to identify the times when they personify the different roles you undertake in everyday life. For example, when I am teaching, explaining things, doing a crossword, working out a cross-stitch design, marking essays or editing written work, I sense that it is Athena-within who is guiding me with her keen intelligence and flair for seeing patterns in things. When I am making something, like bread or a decoration for a festival, and am feeling particularly inspired, I know that it is Brighid-within at work. I know that logic and creativity come from within me, and I choose to identify those parts of myself as Athena, and Brighid, respectively. Identifying them as the Goddess at work within me has helped me to nurture and value these attributes, and has enabled me to summon them up, too, when I need them. This is because, although I know they are already parts of me, I can call upon Athena to bless and guide me when I am writing, and Brighid when I am trying to summon up some inspiration for a project. There are many other examples I could give, but what is important here is that I empower myself by identifying these attributes as 'Goddess-given'. By identifying my Goddesses within, I also identify *myself* as Goddess or Goddesses.

There is a curious and wonderful dynamic that takes place around experiencing the Goddess as aspects of ourselves, then: we can name and identify different aspects of ourselves as Goddesses, and at the same time actively call upon them when we need their power and influence in our lives. The first step, however, is to match aspects of yourself to particular Goddesses. When you have done this, you may feel it necessary to expand your repertoire; this is perfectly feasible, and valid. After all, we do celebrate change — and there is nothing wrong in using or creating something new!

Exercise: Discovering the Inner Goddesses

This exercise is designed to help you identify and match aspects of yourself with various Goddesses, and to consider how you might benefit from their strength and power at different times. It will also invite you to think about different Goddesses that you can call upon, when this is needed. You will need to refer back to the glossary in chapter three for this exercise. You may need to carry out this exercise over a week or so, and come back to it occasionally, as your understanding and experience of the various Goddesses develop.

1   *Using your notebook, jot down the different*
     roles you fulfil in a typical 24-hour period.
     Try thinking of yourself as, for example,
     parent, lover, healer, friend, worker,
     negotiator, carer. Keep it simple at first —
     you can expand this list later, when you have
     more experience of the different Goddesses.

2   *Take these roles one at a time, and imagine*
     yourself into that particular role; what are
     your feelings? How would you describe
     yourself when in that role? What
     characteristics of yourself do you draw upon
     most when 'in role'? Jot down your responses
     next to each role.

3   *Again, taking these roles one at a time, which*
     Goddess do you think is at work here? Try
     searching through the list of different
     Goddesses to identify those who most match
     the role you are considering, and research
     them further, either through the further
     reading recommended at the end of this book,
     or by meditating upon them, and conversing
     with your guiding Goddess.

4   *When you have identified these different*
     Goddesses-within, and feel comfortable with
     your choices, try actively calling upon the
     appropriate Goddess when you need more
     support than usual in a particular role. For
     example, if experiencing difficulty in your

*relationship with your lover, call upon your
love Goddess to remind you that you love this
person, and ask her special guidance. Jot down
the results of doing this, and how you felt —
did you feel more confident, powerful,
competent, etc?*

5   *If your experiment in calling upon your
Goddess did not end as well as you hoped, you
may need to work on your relationship to that
aspect of yourself, or consider it in another
way. Take time out to consider whether you
have actually discovered an aspect of yourself
that needs strengthening, or moderating.*

6   *Return to this exercise as often as you need to
— discovering and calling upon the
Goddess/es within can take a great deal of
practice, but is a very rewarding trail of
discovery!*

The Self as an Aspect of the Goddess

If the Goddess is a part of us, then it is true to say that we are also
Her. Discovering exactly what part of Her we are is one of the most
profound moments of our spiritual journey. For some people, this
discovery is dramatic, and life-changing. For others, it happens
more gradually, and may take a lifetime to discover. There are no
guarantees which way this will go for any individual, and it is up to

us each to accept that there is a truth about our purpose in life that we can find, even if the truth turns out to be the journey itself.

We are all, to some extent or another, components of what we understand as the Goddess. To understand which aspect of Her we are, however, takes a little more exertion. Our efforts to understand, if they are unduly pushy, or the result of stubbornness rather than openness, can sometimes be a barrier, so it is important to approach this in the right frame of mind. One of the first things to do, therefore, is — relax!

It should be stressed at this point that there are no strange notions of 'Universal purpose' being proposed here; the Universe simply already *is*, and, as the song says; 'there ain't nothin'ah cun do about it'! Rather, we are talking about a Goddess of change, and potential for change, and the impact that we have within our own lifetimes, on the life of the planet, and on others. Goddess spirituality is, by and large, more interested in natural change and active change brought about by *agents* (ie people like you and me) rather than any passive notions of 'fate', 'destiny' or 'Divine plans'. The part that you play in positive change, in the realm of sacred possibility, describes which aspect of the Goddess you are.

Exercise: Cosmic Job Description

This exercise can be great fun, but it does have a serious purpose, too. It will help you assess where you are in terms of personal growth, and give you some idea of the role you are playing in your own life and in those of others. Taken more broadly, it can provide an insight into your role on this planet. Use your notebook so that you can refer back to your ideas at a later date, when you are rethinking your 'Cosmic Job Description'.

123

1   Using your notebook, try to write a 'job
     description' for your life as it stands
     presently. This will be easier if you think of it
     as a job that someone else might apply for, if
     you decided suddenly to leave it. What would
     you, or people around you, look for in a
     replacement? Write down a list of 'Essential'
     and 'Desirable' attributes and qualifications,
     as well as a description of the 'job' itself. This
     part of the exercise may take some time!

2   When you have completed your 'Cosmic Job
     Description', go through it carefully and ask
     yourself whether there are some parts of the
     remit that you fit very well and carry out to a
     high standard. Write these down.

3   Looking again at your 'job description', ask
     yourself whether there are some aspects of it
     that you either neglect or do not carry out
     very well. Write these down.

4   Consider your list of tasks and qualities that
     are well fulfilled, and your list of those that
     aren't, and ask yourself whether you are in
     the right 'job'. If you believe that you aren't,
     what might you do to change it?

5   Taking particular note of that part of your
     remit that refers to other people, particular
     parts of the population, or even the planet
     itself, how far is this a reality, and how far an

aspiration? If an aspiration, is this realistic, or desirable? What might be changed, in this case, to accommodate this within your active role?

6   *When you have carried out all of these activities, set some time aside to meditate on which aspect of the Goddess might best describe you. Don't expect miracle revelations at this stage — this is usually a long journey, and this exercise provides the spark that gets you on your way. Remember to do this often, and write down your impressions and thoughts soon after your meditations, so that you can watch your thoughts as they develop.*

7   *Keep a copy of our job description somewhere where you can see it, if possible, to remind yourself of what you think your role is, and whether you are active, or passive in all aspects of it.*

The Goddess as Friend and Confidante

It has already been noted that the relationship between the Goddess and Her people is very different from that encouraged within many mainstream religions. Because we see ourselves as part of Her and Her as part of us, we are free to call upon Her for advice, or just to listen. This doesn't necessarily mean we have no-one else to talk to — Goddess people are a pretty gregarious lot, and rarely lack company. However, there are sometimes occasions or events that we feel we cannot discuss with someone who isn't in our own heads, or feels what we are feeling, and the Goddess, frankly, is the only person who can meet that description.

Goddess people find it utterly natural to call upon the Goddess, or specific Goddesses, at times of stress, pain, anxiety or crisis, because She knows what we are thinking and feeling. When we listen within, we can hear Her, and when we see within, we can see Her nodding, and listening to us. If we are careful to trust our intuition and inner judgement, we can also take advice from Her. Some women have called upon Her to comfort them in childbirth, other men and women have called on Her in grief. Some of us have silent conversations with Her every day, just for the comfort of knowing She is there. Because friendships like this are rarely without their ups and downs, we may even sometimes fall out with Her — or think we do! I remember feeling very shocked when a friend told me that she argued with the Goddess, but recalled later that this 'falling-out' had happened at a time when she herself was being very unreasonable over her relationship with her husband, and their domestic arrangements. She admitted, much later, when things had been resolved, that she was refusing to listen to what her own inner voice was telling her, and the frustration made her lose her temper.

Not all of us may wish to conduct our friendships, or our relationship with the Goddess in quite such a volatile manner(!), but this does point out the very natural and down-to-earth approach to Her that our spiritual path encourages. If we are wilful in ignoring the voice within that tells us that something is wrong, or even right, then we do, strictly speaking 'fall out' with the Goddess in ourselves. This is not a terrible crime, or anything to feel guilty about; it is just a habit we have learned of distrusting the inner voice that is the Goddess. It is, however, a terrible waste of a valuable resource — wisdom.

The Wise Woman

One of the most empowering aspects of the Goddess within is the Old Wise Woman. She is as old as humankind, and as young as the next wise thought that occurs to someone. She is Wise old Grandmother Spider, Thought Woman, the Cailleach, the Crone and Hecate the Witch. She is *La Loba,* the old woman that Clarissa Pinkola Estes found singing over the bones in the desert, and the one who midwifes our unconscious knowledge to birth in our waking consciousness. She is the storyteller who provides us with clues about the truth — the story of our*selves.* The good news is that She is within us all, ancient, crafty, wise and all-knowing.

If we have been brought up, as most of us have, in a system where knowledge and truth are distorted to fit the dominant ideology of the prevailing culture, we have to work a little to allow Her access to our conscious thoughts, and to allow ourselves to attune to Her wisdom. The first step to take is to recognize Her within ourselves.

> *Find the two-million-year-old woman ... She is the mythical voice who knows the past and our ancient history and keeps it recorded for us in stories.*[1]

Fortunately, She offers us this wisdom in symbols and dreams, and tells us the story of ourselves in a way that forces us to develop our all-important intuitive faculties.

If you dream about the Old Woman, listen to what She has to say. It is bound to be important, if not now, then later. If You see Her image in a surrounding culture that denigrates old age and devalues the wisdom of women, do it honour by working to root out prejudice against the bone-deep wisdom that comes from walking 60-plus years on the planet. Better still, do Her honour by finding Her within yourself!

Exercise: Recognizing the Wise-Woman within

This exercise is a visualization, so you should find a space where you will be undisturbed for at least 30 minutes. Remember to jot down any impressions or thoughts in your notebook on emerging from this visualization, as these may come in handy for later reference.

1   *Sit or lie down, whichever is most comfortable, and concentrate on slowing your breathing, and relaxing.*

2   *When you are ready, close your eyes to commence.*

3   *Imagine that it is night-time, and that you are standing before the entrance to a dark, immense cave. The landscape is brown and red, baked earth. The cave is at the foot of a high mountain, that reaches up towards the stars above you. In a bracket immediately inside the entrance is a lit torch. Take the torch from the bracket, and enter the cave.*

4   *Carry on along the passage into the cave, until*
     you can no longer see the entrance, and the
     starry night sky behind you. On the walls
     ahead, in the dark, are bright patches of
     phosphorus, and luminous mosses. Continue
     onwards, down the now gently-declining slope
     of the passage under the mountain.

5   *As you continue, the tunnel grows narrower*
     and more difficult to negotiate. You are still
     able to continue upright, however, and carry
     the torch. The pathway you are travelling
     begins to slope downwards more sharply now,
     and you are deep below the mountain.

6   *Just as a faint light appears ahead of you,*
     your torch goes out, and you continue
     towards the light up ahead. Above you are
     stalactites, rock 'icicles' made by centuries of
     mineral deposits from the underground
     waters that run through the rocks. As you
     near the area of light, you hear something
     rattling.

7   *The area of light is the entrance to a much*
     larger cavern, which is lit with the light of
     millions of luminous mosses, the glowing
     bodies of insects, and the faceted edges of
     quartz crystals. By a pool at the centre of the
     cavern, there is a ring of lit torches, in the
     centre of which sits an old woman, working a
     spinning wheel. She hums a song to the

rhythm of the wheel, and you may catch a few words of her song — take careful note, if you do.

8   *Approach the woman — She knows you are there, and sit before Her as She spins.*

9   *When She is looking at you, ask Her to tell you a story. Listen very carefully to what She has to say.*

10   *Wait until the story is finished, then thank Her and tell Her that you would like to return here often, to hear Her stories. Take careful note of Her response.*

11   *When She goes back to Her spinning, remain seated before Her, and allow the scene to fade around you.*

12   *When you are ready, open your eyes.*

The Goddess as Protector

When Goddess people call upon the Goddess to protect them, they do not mean that we literally expect Her to sweep out of the sky, Boudicca-like, armed to the teeth and ready to do battle with whatever threatens us. Since the Goddess is experienced within, we are calling upon Her to alert us to threats, empower us with fast and appropriate reactions, or help us cast protective spells, and thereby send out our will, our intentions, on the web of magic. Seeing the Goddess of Protection in this way helps us to remember to take care of ourselves, and also offers us a very real power to draw upon when we need to defend ourselves. Sad to say, we live in a dangerous world, where we need to be alert to all forms of danger — including that of attack by a violent person. Wearing a Goddess symbol around your neck as a talisman is not going to guarantee immunity from this — but empowering yourself and taking sensible precautions may. This is when the Goddess of Protection really swings into action.

Activists in the Goddess movement have long recognized the power of invoking and conjuring up symbols, images and Goddesses in order to defend themselves and others. The image of the Medusa, the snake-haired Gorgon, has been used since the early 1970s as a powerful feminist symbol.[2] Images of Boudicca, the warrior Queen, Amazons, and Artemis have been used as tools of empowerment in the women's movement over the last 30 years. The Goddess-symbol of the web was put to good use in women's anti-nuclear protests, and symbols of females traditionally considered as monstrous in patriarchal culture, such as Two Headed Women,[3] have been re-appropriated and used for positive empowerment. The invocation of a powerful Goddess protector at times of crisis can also be a personal matter. I have experienced a moment of extreme anger when a 'flasher' exposed himself to me in a park, as I was walking to work. Instead of running away, or reacting with disgust (which I am sure he expected), I roared at him with sheer outrage at this abusive act, and chased him when he ran off in shock. Later, I recognized that this was the Gorgon, and I was drawing on Gorgon power to express my — and many women's — rage against this form of violation. I was interested to read later, that other women had experienced Gorgon power, too,[4] and have kept Her nourished and cared for within me ever since!

Being able to draw upon the Goddess/es within is a good form of protection. Drawing on the Wise Woman within helps us access our deep knowledge, our intuition. That intuition can be literally life-saving in some circumstances, and encourages us to listen to our physical, psychological and emotional responses to situations that *something in us knows* is potentially dangerous. Our inner Goddesses *know* when something is wrong, when the house is too quiet, when a stranger or even an acquaintance is acting oddly. The Gorgon, however, empowers us to react appropriately.

Exercise: Discovering the Inner Gorgon

This exercise will help you to find your Gorgon — your inner wild and angry woman. Because many of us have been taught that anger is wrong, or destructive, this exercise may seem a little difficult, so don't worry if you have to repeat it a couple of times, or come back to it when you feel more ready. You will need to be very honest with yourself in order to track down your Gorgon, so don't cheat by trying to give 'nice' answers!

1   *Using your notebook, write down as many things that make you* really *angry as you can.*

2   *When you have done this, go back through the list and strike out any of the ones you think of as manageable, or less important, eg people leaving the cap off the toothpaste, or leaving the toilet seat up.*

3   *Turning to the remaining items on your list, tick those that you think are due to unreasonable prejudice, your own personal*

likes and dislikes, and any that seem trivial against larger issues. These should now be crossed off this list, but written up as a separate personal list so that you can revisit them at some time — they are not trivial to you, of course, as they would not have survived the first stage of elimination if they were. These are for you to work through at a future time, when you are ready.

4 *Items on your list should now read something like a list of what you think is wrong in the world — a list of injustices. Put down your pen for a moment, and concentrate on how each of these injustices make you feel.*

5 *Close your eyes and mix all of these feelings together. Imagine yourself mixing them in a big cauldron.*

6 *When they are mixed, say aloud; I bid the Gorgon, rise! and watch as your Gorgon climbs out of the cauldron.*

7 *Look at the Gorgon carefully — do you feel threatened by Her? Don't! She is a part of you, and cannot bid you to do things you don't wish to, or be set loose to create chaos without you. Allow Her to merge with you, and allow your anger to die down.*

8   *Your first meeting with your Gorgon may
     make you feel odd. Don't worry — it is
     perfectly normal. If you still feel angry at the
     end of this exercise, you should eat and drink,
     and perform a useful physical task, such as
     gardening, or exercise. Then, before you go to
     sleep at night, imagine your anger climbing
     back into the cauldron, and melting again.*

9   *You can draw upon the Gorgon when you
     need Her — She will help you focus your
     anger in order to put it to positive use.
     Remember, anger is natural in an unnatural
     world — so don't be afraid of your own. You
     will find, with the Gorgon's help, ways of
     putting it to good use.*

Fairytales and Legends

You will probably be surprised to learn that you already had a
wealth of symbols and images to draw upon for invoking the
Goddess within, before you even opened this book. You may, if
you approach them from a Goddess-perspective, recognize Her in
fairytales as well as some of the myths and legends you have
encountered from childhood. Most of us are familiar with the figure
of the innocent young woman, the mother, the witch, the old
woman and various Goddesses from European, Australian, African
and American fairytales and myths. The old woman who tests the
kind-heartedness of various heroes and heroines, the kind fairy
godmother who advises various forlorn maidens, or threatened

children: all of these are images that have some resonance within Goddess spirituality.

The value of reclaiming and recreating female figures from old myths and stories was discovered early on by the women's movement in the 1970s, and by the Goddess spirituality movement from the beginning. Women recognized the need to reclaim female figures and Goddesses from patriarchal myths. Finding symbols of the Goddess in fairytales and familiar myths is not without problems, admittedly. Some of the most popular fairytales in the west have come down to us after considerable 'cutting and pasting'. This is particularly true of Perrault's 17th-century aristocratic tales for the French Court, and of the Brothers Grimm's drastic subversion of the oral traditions of central Germany.[5] In addition, the Greek myths handed down to us were not original tales of the Goddesses, but created by a predominantly patriarchal and misogynistic society.[6] However, there are still many valuable symbols to draw from familiar tales, to inspire us in our own storytelling. Although we are denied easy access to many of the original stories told about Goddesses, we can find clues, and make new ones from them — stories that are relevant to us now.

Not everybody likes the idea of people re-writing familiar stories, or creating tales that see women in a more holistic, positive light — but in truth, if the old stories are oppressive, and continue to feed distorted ideas about women and men, why shouldn't we? After all, at some point somebody had to write down the old stories for the first time! In actual fact, there is very little 'purity' in contemporary popular fairytales, which have altered so much since they were taken from the peasantry and written down by those from the more privileged classes, that they bear almost no relation to their originals. Many of them, for example, were drastically changed and

135

Christianized by the Grimms, to provide moralistic tales aimed at indoctrinating young children with a harsh notion of 'good' behaviour. Taking the lead, therefore, from Monica Wittig's invitation to 'remember ... or failing that, invent', it is difficult to see why we shouldn't reclaim stories and fairytales for ourselves, or even write new ones!

Judith Plaskow writes of her Goddess group's rewriting of the myth of Adam and Eve, entitled 'The Coming of Lilith':

> *We had a journey to go on, an enemy (or enemies)*
> *to vanquish, salvation to be achieved both for*
> *ourselves and for humanity.*[7]

In their story, they chose to retell the story of the garden of Eden, but beginning with Lilith, a figure demonized within Jewish mythology, as Adam's first wife. By re-diverting the actions of the main characters, and inserting the figure of Lilith, they were able to tell a different story, one that came out of the experiences of the women in the group, and which made sense to them. Another 'myth-activist', Charlene Spretnak, decided to actively reclaim the Greek myths using, as far as possible, archaeological evidence from the pre-Hellenic era, in order to trace and piece together the surviving fragments of the Goddesses' original functions, prior to their being 'paired' with superior male Gods. Her stories keep some of the Goddesses' more positive attributes of the Greek myths, but weave in the extra information, and inspiration, taken from the pre-Hellenic evidence. Her stories of the Goddesses subvert the very distorted view of women offered in the Greek myths, and offer a more empowering mythology. In Spretnak's version, for example, Pandora is a gift-*giver* (a valid, alternative interpretation of her name), rather than one whose curiosity led to all sorts of ills coming into the world — rather like Eve's function in Genesis. In Spretnak's Goddess-centred stories, the tale of Demeter and Persephone becomes a tale of love between mother and daughter, and Persephone's discovery of life, rather than a tale of rape and abduction.[8]

As you can see, using our creative imaginations to reclaim and rewrite familiar myths and stories can be a liberating experience! Invoking symbols from our childhood and then weaving them into stories that re-define them — and us — is extremely empowering. For this skill, we can draw upon Grandmother Spider, the great storyteller Herself. It is She, after all, who whispers to us in our dreams, and makes the hairs on our neck stand up, or makes us feel things 'in our bones', when She is telling us the true story of ourselves. Her wisdom and skill are already within us — if we are prepared to look.

Exercise: Goddess Stories as Personal Empowerment

This exercise will demonstrate how it is possible to create new stories from old in an empowering way. The exercise is in two parts, the first refers to the story below, and the second relates to writing your own Goddess-centred story.

Firstly, read through the story below twice, the first time without taking notes, and the second time, making notes guided by the prompts that follow afterwards. Keep your notes, to return to from time to time when you wish to review your responses, or have new ideas to add.

The Story of the Singing Jar

Once upon a time, when the world was old but humankind was still young, there lived a singularly-blessed being by the name of Cassandra. Cassandra not only never told a lie — she was the very essence of truth, and could not be held back from being honest and saying what She saw, wherever She was, and in whatever company. She was highly honoured among the people, and often called upon and asked for the truth about this or that. With Cassandra to guide them, the people soon became so adept at recognizing the truth for themselves that She felt able to leave them for a while, and went to live in the mountains, to play with Her sisters all day, and weave, sew and throw and paint beautiful pots.

After She had been in the mountains for a couple of thousand years, She started to feel uneasy. Sometimes, in the middle of the night, Cassandra was disturbed by echoes that sounded like cries for help. Sometimes, in the middle of the day, She saw mirages of scenes of suffering. After a while, She set off down the mountain with a magical jar to give as a gift to the first humans She met. She filled it with clear mountain water to sustain Her on the journey, strapped it onto Her shoulders, and set off down the mountain, to see how the humans were coping.

When She reached the first village at the foot of the mountain, She was amazed to find that nobody recognized her. When She announced Her presence, people shrugged and walked past Her, though some had the good grace to look embarrassed. She noticed that things in the village had changed somewhat, too. Some of the humans wore better clothing than others, and some thin and worried-looking humans scurried about, waiting on the ones who were smartly dressed and well-fed. Cassandra noticed that the women no longer sang at the well, but stayed indoors, whilst some of the men wandered about at will, lording it over other men. She was horrified to see some humans in chains, with the scars of beatings, and some children cower away from the adults. What She noticed most of all, however, was the all-pervading smell of Fear.

Cassandra stood in the middle of the village, and took a long swig of the mountain water, to clear Her throat before speaking. She placed the empty jar on the ground at Her feet, and called for the village to assemble. They did not come forward, however, but retreated to their homes. Cassandra was left alone, in the full glare of the noonday sun, to tell Her truth to anyone who might be listening from their huts. Her voice rang through every door, wall and roof, and even people who put their fingers in their ears could hear Her clear voice. She began by telling the truth about the slaves that She saw in the village, naming them as human beings who could be owned by no-one. She told the truth about the cowering children, who were living under the domination of adults, and taught by fear instead of love, and then She told the truth about the rich and the poor, and how there was plenty for all, if only it were shared out fairly. Last of all, She saved Her most sorrowful tale for the women, at whom She directed the truth about their miserable state of submission.

After a long silence, the head man of the village came out, told Cassandra that She should be ashamed at such lies, and told her to leave. However, She continued to tell the truth to the head man about his swaggering and bullying as head of the village. He became enraged, and warned Her that She had better leave before he had Her thrown out. He stalked off, leaving Cassandra to continue to tell the truth about the unhappiness She saw.

Soon, a woman, her head and face hidden by a shawl, crept out of a house and came to talk to her. 'Go away,' she hissed, half in anger, half in fear, 'you're making trouble for us. The big people will take it out on the slaves and the women and children. It's alright for you — you can leave at any time.' Cassandra looked at her in amazement, and asked, 'How could things possibly be worse than they already are? You all live in fear and misery and worry in case you are punished just for existing. What could be worst than that?' The woman knew the truth of this, but instead of taking courage from it, became more afraid than ever, and in her anger, kicked Cassandra's jar over. As the jar broke, Cassandra disappeared into a million fragments, carried off by the wind, each one of them sighing in despair. At this sound, all of the villagers came running out to see what had happened. The woman, afraid of what she had seen, told them that Cassandra had disappeared, and everyone, even the slaves, heaved a sigh of relief. Cassandra's presence had made them all uncomfortable. Soon, the villagers lost interest, and drifted back to their huts.

The woman who had broken the jar, however, noticed a small child picking up the pieces, and trying to put them together again. She stopped to help him, and soon a slave joined them in picking up the fragments of the shattered jar. The woman, the child and the slave worked together all through the night, reassembling the jar. They glued it with tree-gum, and as they worked, began to whisper together about the state of affairs in the village. Towards dawn, the jar was entirely mended, and when the final piece was glued in place, it magically became whole, without a sign or line of its breakage to be seen. Startled by this sudden transformation, and growing afraid of the truths they had whispered to each other, the three ran off to their huts.

At dawn, as the sun rose, a wind blew down the mountain, calling for Cassandra to return. The wind entered the mouth of the jar, and the jar began to sing. The villagers were roused by the sound, and crept towards the jar just as soon as curiosity overcame fear. At first they could not hear what the jar was saying, so they had to approach it very closely. As soon as the first woman approached it, the truth leapt from the jar and into her mouth, and she was immediately aware that she was compelled to tell the truth for all time. She put her hand over her mouth to stop it getting out, and to save herself from getting into so-ooo much trouble. Seeing her look of terror, and taking it for surprise, the villagers drew closer to the jar to see what had caused her to startle and leap back. As they did, the truth leapt out into various mouths. It leapt into the mouth of a slave, a child, a poor man, and a woman, and each time their hands flew to their mouths. Every person in the village who was ruled over in some way by somebody else found themselves compelled to tell the truth when they approached the jar.

After a while, the rulers amongst them tried in vain to bury the jar in the mountains, but the wind must have blown the top-soil away, for every so often, when the wind blows down the mountain and catches in the mouth of the jar, Cassandra's voice is heard, telling the truth. Those who hear it immediately clap their hands over their mouths, just like the villagers. However, like the villagers, they can't hold their hand over their mouth forever, and the truth, as they say, will out.

1   *Using a dictionary of Classical references, a book of Greek myths or an internet search, try to find out what Greek mythology has to say about the story of the prophetess Cassandra. In which important ways does it differ from the story above?*

141

2   *In the story above, why, do you think, were the slaves, the children and the women so afraid of what Cassandra had to say?*

3   *Have you, or anyone else you know, ever been called a 'Cassandra'? Does this expression fit with what you now understand Cassandra to be, having read this story?*

4   *Where can Cassandra be seen in action presently in the world? Can you identify her presence in particular people, or groups of people either now or at different moments in history?*

5   *Under what circumstances might you wish to invoke Cassandra-within? What sort of things do you think She might help you to do? In which ways might you find Her empowering to you personally?*

6   *Can you identify points in your life where being able to identify Cassandra-within would have helped you? How do you feel about those circumstances now?*

The next part of this exercise is about writing your own story. Choose a myth, a fairytale, or a Goddess or female figure from either, and write a story based around it/Her from a Goddess-centred perspective. This means from a 'Cassandra' point of view — revealing a truth about the story or the figure! You may find it useful to choose some of the components of storytelling from the list below, just to get you started. These are not in any particular order, so pick whichever ones you need. Not all of the components are necessary — feel free to choose some and leave out others, according to your own wishes.

Goddess	journey	complication
female figure	gift	difficulty to be overcome
magical object	problem	solution
quest	time	place
friend	opposing force/s	special powers
helpers	object of desire	hidden truth

When you have written your story, honour the spirit of creativity that helped you write it, by reading it aloud in a candlelit room, either to yourself, or to a friend, or group of friends you know will appreciate it. If you are thinking about working in a group (see chapter seven), getting people in the group to write and tell empowering Goddess-stories is a good exercise to help you explore your own spirituality, and to share ideas with others. In this way, storytelling becomes not only personal empowerment, but collective knowledge from which many people can draw encouragement and wisdom.

As you can see, there are many different ways to discover the Goddess within — She has never been very far away! Although we may have to exert ourselves at first to find Her, it becomes easier over time to for us to recognize Her within ourselves and others, and call Her up when we need Her. Blessings Be on the Goddess you are!

Notes

1   Pinkola Estes, 1992, page 34.

2   Caputi, in Larrington, 1992, page 431.

3   Walker, 1988, pages 1—2.

4   Caputi in Larrington, 1992, page 431.

5   Bottigheimer, 1987.

6   Spretnak, 1992.

7   Plaskow, in Christ and Plaskow, 1992, page 205.

8   Spretnak, 1992, pages 53—57 and 105—118.

SIX

THE GODDESS
of Change

So far, this book has referred to the Goddess, and Goddess spirituality, as being about change. It has spoken about the discernible changes that take place in nature, the changes that take place throughout the human life-cycle, and the cycle of eternal change that is found throughout the Universe. However, the Goddess is also a Goddess of changes brought about by action, through the agency of humans who have heard Cassandra's song of truth coming from the singing jar. There are many human beings who are truly touched with the inspiration and courage to make the world a better place for others. They rarely experience the world as a better place for themselves, because they tell the truth, and this is rarely rewarded with a comfortable, or safe existence in many parts of the world. These are the heroes and heras of change — the Rosa Parks of the world, who refuse to give their seat to a white person simply because they are black, the Sylvia Pankhursts, who suffer violence and oppression because they believe that women have rights, and refuse to accept otherwise. But there are other types of heroes and heras, too, of the everyday type, who struggle for positive change in the world, and try to defend the planet against violence and destruction. These are also sons and daughters of the Goddess of Change, and every bit as courageous in their own way as those who make symbolic or dramatic gestures to force change into being.

There is another sense, too, in which the Goddess of Change can touch our lives, and that is in our personal lives. When we are unhappy because of the way that we are living, whether inflicted by others, or because we don't 'fit' the life in which we thought we would find contentment, we can call upon the Goddess to help us change things. There is no promise that this will be easy, and it certainly won't be instant or miraculous, but with the Goddess of Change in your corner, many things become possible that may not even have entered your frame of reference before. It has been noticed in the Goddess community, that when men and women set off on the path, they often find their lives changing, sometimes quite dramatically. Some break away from old relationships and form new ones. Others grow a wholly different relationship with their children, or their parents, and wise up to false 'friends' or acquaintances who drain their energy without ever giving anything back. Other friendships will be strengthened, and cherished as the people in them come to see how valuable they are. This reconfiguration of the relationships in their life is not a result of a 'curse' that makes you selfish because you are discovering your own spiritual potential — rather it is a consequence of self-realization, re-valuing your own needs, and listening to Cassandra's singing jar.

The Goddess of Change supports these life-shifts, most of which happen gradually, some of which will seem to your old friends and acquaintances to have happened 'suddenly'. Suffice to say that, if relationships are already happy and solid, nothing, especially spiritual development, can harm them. If anything, they will be enhanced by the positive changes that take place within a person. If they are shaky, however, a strong dose of the truth will either transform them, or dispose of them altogether.

As we come to value ourselves more, we also come to value others, too, and support them in their personal journeys. Some religious paths demand a life of 'sacrifice' from their followers, and consequently, self-care and self-value are seen within that worldview as selfish or vain. In Goddess spirituality, caring for ourselves is a duty we owe to ourselves — if we *are* the Goddess, then we really should honour and take care of ourselves! We help others because it is the right thing to do — not because we are considered bad if we don't also do things for others. On the great web of existence, an injury to one is an injury to all, so many of us work against injustice in

147

different ways, every day. However, to help others does not mean to neglect or sacrifice ourselves — if we are all part of the same thing, there is little to be gained from destroying one part of the web — ourselves — in order to save another — also ourselves! So there is no contradiction in Goddess spirituality, in looking after ourselves, and each other, in order to bring about positive personal, and wider, changes.

Many political activists find themselves in danger of 'burnout' when they throw their energies into a campaign, without stopping to 'refuel' with rest, nourishment and self-care every now and again. The web is not a better place for having teachers, social workers, carers and activists who burn out and break down — it is a better place for having teachers, social workers, carers and activists who continue to function. The Goddess of Change is also a Goddess of Healing — and on a world-wide scale that means bringing things into a natural, fair and just balance. This can be pretty wearing on the people who are pro-active in this project, and as Alex Plows, a well-known green activist has pointed out: 'We have busy lives, but remember that the person is political. Take care of yourself.'[1] The Goddess of Change does not demand 'burnout' of us — remember, She is a Goddess of healing, and that applies as much to the individual as it does to the whole.

The Green Goddess and the Environment

The Goddess of the environment is the Green Goddess — the Spirit of all nature, and the land. Some Goddess people will talk about the 'rape of the Earth', whilst others will recoil from using a phrase that they find ill-fitting and not particularly productive. Not all of us are happy to speak of the earth as a woman, since this paints women as passive, exploitable, and essentializes us as beings ruled by what our oppressors have deemed our 'biological destiny' — ie fertility. However, we do recognize a Green Goddess who manifests as the demand for justice to, and balance in, nature. We serve Her, and ourselves, by being energy-conscious and pollution-aware in our everyday lives. We join campaigns, sometimes in a small, and sometimes in a bigger, more active way, to find ways of saving the environment from destruction. Our planet is a web of life whose delicate balance humans are threatening to overthrow — and the Green Goddess calls to us in our dreams, through the hole we have created in the ozone layer, with a wake-up call to galvanize us into finding a solution.

Many Goddess people can be described as having an 'ecofeminist' spirituality. This means that they are spiritually and practically aware of the damage being done to nature, considered as sacred, through their consciousness of various other oppressions, including the oppression of women. It is generally recognized within spiritual ecofeminism that the destruction of nature comes out of a similar sort of thinking as the oppression of some groups of people by others. This idea, that humans can dominate nature, that men can dominate women, whites can dominate people of colour, etc, describes a mindset that is prevalent within patriarchal societies. In fact, you will meet this way of thinking in a variety of different, and more sophisticated scenarios throughout the world. This sort of thinking is the opposite of that found within Goddess conscious-ness. The Green Goddess of the environment speaks of equality, balance and justice — all life-affirming, people- and nature-friendly concepts. The sort of logic where some things rule over others, how-ever, consists of death-affirming, people- and nature-destructive concepts.

In the case of nature, spiritual ecofeminists see humans using the earth as an endless resource, and polluting it as we exploit it. The cause of profit has been put above the basic truth about the damage that is already affecting us, and the ultimate consequence of a dying earth, if things continue in this way. This is sometimes very complex, especially where pollution and environmental destruction equals construction work for people who have no other income, and this makes the environmental message unpopular. Once again, Goddess people and other activists are forced to speak from the mouth of Cassandra's jar — and consequently suffer for it.

Some activists, however, especially those who are inspired by 'eco-magic' — the magic to be found around us in nature and used for the good of the earth — can draw upon the power of the Goddess of the Land. She may be conceived of as Dragon Power, or Serpent Power, depicted as a Gorgon or a Hydra — but She is still the Goddess of the Land, rising to empower those who wish to defend the Earth. Some activists draw the Goddess of the Land into them-selves to confound the destroyers — painting themselves with mud, wearing wigs of grass, straw and leaves, and invoking Her power. Others weave webs around bases and complexes where violence and pollution in potential are stored. All these actions are inspired by the Spirit of all Nature; the Green Goddess of the environment.

Exercise: Meeting the Green Goddess

This exercise is a visualization, so you will need to find a place where you will be undisturbed for at least 30 minutes.

1   *Sit or lie down, whichever is the most*
    comfortable, and concentrate on slowing your
    breathing, and relaxing.

2   *When you are ready to commence, close your eyes.*

3   *Sink into the darkness behind your eyelids, and imagine that you are standing on a sandy shore, in front of a green, tranquil sea. Waves are washing gently at your feet, and all around you are sand, rocks and shells. Spend a while watching the waves lap against the shore, feeling the warmth of the sun on your skin, and smelling the scent of salt water, fish and seaweed.*

4   *In the distance, a small boat approaches. It is without crew, and the rudder appears to be directing itself towards you. As the little boat approaches, you see that it has a single white sail, and eyes painted on its prow. The boat comes very close to you. Wade into the water, and step in.*

5   *The boat reverses out, this time with you on board, sitting on one of the wooden plank seats, and turns, its prow pointing seawards. The wind catches in the little sail, and the boat sets off at some speed over the water, with you facing forwards.*

6   *After a short space of time, the shore behind you recedes, until no land is visible at all. The Sun beats down, and the wind pushes the boat onwards, until you spot a distant shore. As*

you approach, you see that it is a small island, with a hill, woods, and streams and waterfalls flowing over the small cliffs and rocks, into the sea.

7   *Eventually, the boat touches shore, and you jump out, onto a beach of white sand, studded with pearls and beautiful pink shells. The cliffs are patterned with the different colours of the age of the rock — layers all compressed into different seams, now shining in the sun as quartz, amethyst, coal, amber, gold, silver, copper and all types and colours of rock. The trees are as various as they are numerous — there are palms and yuccas, as well as oaks and blackthorns. Bushes lining the shore are all in fruit and flower at the same time, and hummingbirds and bees flit amongst them, whilst above, on the hills, are deer and soaring eagles.*

8   *You proceed towards a clearing in the woods, marvelling at the variety of life around you, and listening for the crashes of apes and bears in the undergrowth. As you find a path through the trees, you will hear the exquisite song of thousands of different birds, and the distant howl of wolves on the hillsides. The pathway is lined with thousands of tiny candles, and you follow it upwards, as it climbs towards a dark clearing in the undergrowth.*

9 *The clearing, as you near it, is dark because of the canopy of the forest roof above it. It holds a building, very much like a temple, made of various types of marble — black, pink, green and white. The door is very ancient oak, and as you step towards it, it swings inwards in welcome.*

10 *As you enter the temple, the door closes behind you, and you find yourself standing in a circular space, lit only by the daylight entering a solar skylight in the centre of the roof. You move to the centre, and stand directly in the beam of sunlight in the middle of the room. At first, the light is a little blinding, but as your eyes become accustomed to it, you notice for the first time a figure coming towards you.*

11 *The figure is a mature woman, dressed in green and carrying a large wrought-iron pentagram. Smiling kindly, She offers it to you. Take it.*

12 *The pentagram is so heavy that you feel overcome by the weight, but at the same time, you are still able to hold it. The Goddess makes a gesture, and the pentagram rises vertically into the beam of light, unhindered by gravity, and spinning upright on its diametric axis. It tilts gently, and spins faster and faster until it becomes a globe. The globe*

*is blue, white, green and brown. It looks like a
school-child's globe of the world, but when
you inspect it more closely, you see that the
waters are moving, and the clouds forming
and reforming. You see weather fronts moving
across its face, and parts of the ice-caps
breaking away. You are looking at planet
Earth.*

13   *The Goddess is showing you the planet, your
home. It is a thing of perfect beauty, until
something strange begins to happen. The ice
caps melt, the waters rise, the forests shrink,
and in places the Earth is scorched. In fast
motion, you are being shown the damage it
has taken humans about 500 years to inflict.*

14   *The Goddess looks directly at you,
questioningly — what can be done?*

15   *Ask Her what you can do to help within your
own life, and listen carefully while She tells
you.*

16   *When you are ready, allow the scene around
you to fade, and open your eyes. Make a note
of your impressions, anything of importance
that was said, or seen, before you get
something to eat or drink.*

17   *In the weeks that follow this exercise, you can connect again with the Green Goddess in the following ways:*

Go to a green spot near your home, where you will be undisturbed, and sit on the ground, with your back against a tree if possible, and try to feel the deep pulse of life all around you.

Light a green candle each evening for one moon cycle, to honour the Green Goddess, and begin to decorate your home with living, green plants.

Explore and research different Goddesses of Earth and growth, and learn about the stone circles, sacred sites and burial places of the ancient peoples where you live. If you are lucky enough to visit these, spend some time trying to 'tune in' to the spirit of the place, and of the land, where these sites were constructed.

Be practical, beginning in small ways, by finding out how to save water, conserve energy and recycle glass, paper, cans in your home and in the neighbourhood.

Encountering Changing Woman

Changing Woman is a Navajo Goddess of change and renewal, some-times known as 'Estsanatlehi'. In the Chiricahua Apache tradition, she is also known as Painted Woman. She is a personification of the changes of the Earth, and is renowned also for her ability to change Herself: when She grows old, She walks towards the East, the place of the rising sun, and meets Her young self walking towards Her. She merges with Her young self, turns around, and comes back renewed and invigorated. In Goddess spirituality, references to 'Changing Woman' are often used when invoking the ability to change from within, and giving power to changes we are trying to make in the world around us. We also call upon Her shape-shifting energy, which is raised in the casting of magical spells for change. One of the most popular chants in the Goddess spirituality movement was created by the Reclaiming Collective, a US-based group, and is invoked whenever we wish to invoke change, or simply honour Changing Woman:

> *She changes everything She touches,*
> *And everything She touches changes*

The alterations that the energy of Changing Woman can make often come gradually, like the erosion and reshaping of stones by water. This means that the change is non-violent, sustainable, and perma-nent. Changing Woman is a symbol and an energy within Goddess spirituality, used to encourage us to effect change *actively*. As you have already learned, we acknowledge the changes in life and in the world around us that happen in the course of nature. But we also hold that we can be agents of change, too, if we become active weavers and transformers. Changing Woman is a Goddess of Transformation — a Goddess of the magic of change that can be rendered by the activities of human beings.

There are, broadly speaking, three different ways in which change is actively initiated and sustained within Goddess spirituality. The first of these is *inner* change, which can be initiated by visualization, active learning (reading and participating in educative exercises), and direct experience. The second of these is *outer* change initiated by ritual and magic, worked either solo, or in a group. The third is *outer* change initiated and sustained through practical, everyday work and action. Needless to say, all of these are interconnected, even when one way seems to take on more emphasis than the others. In the course of the next three chapters, you will learn more about working rituals and casting spells in sacred space, and discovering your own powers of transformation. In the meantime, you are encouraged to carry out the exercise below, which is a simple ritual to ask Changing Woman to come into your life. Part of the ritual is a form of self-blessing to set you off on your journey, and it is a lovely ceremony to initiate inner change, and introduce you to ritual in Goddess spirituality. I hope you enjoy it.

Exercise: Changing Woman Ritual

The object of this ritual is to invoke Changing Woman to initiate changes within you, to prepare you for the spiritual work in everyday life, rituals and magic. You will need to find a place where you will be undisturbed for at least an hour. You will need one white household candle, four tea-lights, or votives, in safe containers, a piece of turquoise if you can get it, or an item that is turquoise in colour, a packet of salt with a small opening in the top for pouring. This ritual is best carried out after dark, or at dawn and, if possible (though not essential), at Dark Moon.

1   *Prior to the ritual, prepare the area in which you will work, placing the white household*

*candle in a safe holder in the centre of the
floor, and the four tea-lights in safe places at
equal distances from each other around the
room at cardinal points of the compass —
North, South, East and West. Place the
turquoise, or the turquoise item, in the centre
with the white candle.*

2   *Before the ritual, bathe or shower, and enter
the space in which you will work either naked,
or in a simple robe.*

3   *Take the salt, and pour it in a circle all around
you on the floor, so that the four white
candles stand at each quarter. Keep the salt
with you in the centre of the circle.*

4   *When this is done, light the tea-light in the
East, saying:* Walking East towards the
sunrise, I meet myself.

Light the tea-light in the South, saying:
Walking South towards noon, I meet the
infinite Sun.

Light the tea-light in the West, saying:
Walking West towards the sunset, I meet the
Waters.

Light the tea-light in the North, saying:
Walking North towards midnight, I meet the
Earth.

Light the white candle in the centre, saying:
Walking towards Spirit, I meet Changing
Woman.

5   *Sit down in the centre of the circle, and hold*
the turquoise, or turquoise item in your
hands. Close your eyes and breathe deeply for
at least a hundred heartbeats. While you do
this, think about the words you have said at
each candle, and what they mean to you.

6   *Open your eyes, place the turquoise, or item,*
in front of the candle, and raise your hands
before you, palms turned slightly upwards in
a gesture of welcome, and invoke Changing
Woman to come to you, saying slowly and
clearly:

Changing Woman, Goddess of constant change
    and transformation,
Hear me
I am ready to begin
I am ready to change
I am ready to be a weaver of change
I am ready to hear your voice
I am ready to speak your words.
Hear me
Changing Woman, Goddess of constant change
    and transformation

7   *Stay in this position, and try to sense the*
energies within and around you.

8   When you are ready, stand up and pour a lit-
     tle salt on the ground between you and the
     candle. Step forward onto the salt, and say:

     As I step onto Earth,
     I become like the Earth,
     As the Earth turns and changes,
     I become like the Earth.
     Changing Woman,
     As I bless you
     I bless myself.
     Blessed Be.

9   Close your eyes, and concentrate on the image
     of the lit candle behind your eyelids. Allow the
     Changing Woman energies to course through
     your body, and open yourself to Her spirit
     working in you.

10   When you are ready, open your eyes and sit in
     the circle for a while, in silence, and allow any
     thoughts or impressions to flow, unhindered.
     Spend as long as you wish in this way, and
     enjoy the peace and stillness.

11   Close your ritual by extinguishing the candle
     and tea-lights, and scuffing the boundaries of
     the salt circle with your foot. You can vacuum
     up the salt at your earliest convenience, but
     keep the turquoise, or turquoise item, where
     you can see it in your room for at least one
     moon cycle.

*12   Write up in your notebook any impressions or
thoughts that came to you in the circle. You
will not always make notes after rituals, but
until you get used to processing thoughts and
impressions, it is a useful reference tool.*

Goddess of Inspiration, Hope and Empowerment

When we are actively seeking to make changes around us, we can
call upon the Goddess to give us the energy we need to support our
just causes. As pointed out earlier, when the women's movement
reclaimed Goddess symbols from patriarchy, they put them to good
use in inspirational writing, and as emblems of campaigns. The
Goddess spirituality movement takes this a few steps further. For us,
identifying ourselves with the Goddess/es means that we can evolve
our own personal mythologies, and empower ourselves with
Her/their energy/ies as we set about actively creating change within
and around us.

The changes that take place within us are hard to quantify or explain
to outsiders by their very nature. Only we are to know if calling upon
Isis helped us in our attitude towards the healing process when we
were sick, or that invoking Artemis in a relationship crisis helped us
retain our dignity and independence as that relationship crumbled.
We can, to a certain extent, share this secret with sympathetic
friends, but the experience and nature of our relationship with different Goddesses is profoundly personal. However inwardly they are
experienced, our personal relationships with our inner Goddesses
impact on our lives in a real and palpable way. For example, people
who are timid, and get used to drawing upon Kali to lend Her fiery

courage, find that by calling upon Her often, they nurture the part of them that was difficult to summon, and consequently, their timidity diminishes. People who know they are liable to irritable unreasonableness and flashes of temper, and call frequently upon Rhiannon to lend balance, may find themselves growing naturally more reasonable and calm. In calling upon the Goddess/es to energize a particular aspect of our characters, we effectively nourish that part of us, and are changed by it.

Changes that take place around us, through invocation of the Goddess/es, are not as easy to pinpoint as one may imagine, either. It can only be said that where we see the changes in question as being a consequence of the Goddess at work in some way, then that is what it is to *us*. However, some work towards outward change can be experienced through something that happens to us inwardly when we invoke the power and strength of the Goddess. Some environmental campaigners have invoked the Goddess of Earth in the form of a dragon, before protesting peacefully and non-violently before people who they know are not peaceful and non-violent. One woman described this as, 'a rush of energy that filled me with the feeling that I had to perform a dance of defiance in front of these people'. In fact, some protesters have used the invocation of Goddess and Earth power as a non-violent weapon against the destroyers. The woman who felt inspired to dance her defiance smeared mud on her face, along with several others, and they shrieked and danced in front of their opponents, who stopped in their tracks in amazement. Some found this 'sacred madness' too unnerving, and refused to move any further towards the protesters, which was exactly the desired effect! The Goddess can inspire, raise hope, and empower us to change things positively, and without the violence that characterizes the forces of destruction that threaten the Earth and its people.

It may seem to us that the Goddess of Change works in mysterious ways. But She works in ways that we can experience personally, communally, and in a wider sense, politically. For Goddess people, change is not only a natural consequence of being alive and in touch with the world, but is something we *cause*, too. For those of us who wish to cause positive changes, the power of the Goddess of Change is crucial, as it is Her energy that we draw upon in order to inspire not only ourselves, but others. With Changing Woman in our corner, the miracle of lasting change in the everyday world is made possible, both within and around us.

Notes

1   Plows, in *Dragon*, Spring issue, 2001.

SEVEN

EVERYDAY
Spirituality

Goddess spirituality is everyday spirituality. We don't have, as a rule, temples to attend on certain days of the week, or at special festivals, but instead integrate our spirituality into our everyday lives. Although we do occasionally feel the need to create what we call 'sacred space' in which to meditate, cast spells or perform rituals, this is usually created in our own homes, in spaces that are returned to their customary function immediately after. As you would expect from a spirituality that is so keen on inter-connection, our spiritual lives are not reserved or held back, to be brought out on particular occasions, but are part of our everyday selves. Accordingly, some of us like to surround ourselves with things that are affirmative of our spirituality, for example, symbols or images that we find personally meaningful and empowering.

Another aspect of an integrated spirituality is that it enables us to call upon our inner resources during everyday life, wherever we are, and whatever we are doing. This means that during a particularly stressful day, we can call up our inner self-defence system, perhaps in the shape of a particular Goddess or symbol. We can also help to create a supportive, co-operative environment in the place that we work, whether this is in the home or in a busy office, by importing particular symbols, or working a little magic.

One way in which we connect with the cycles of nature on an everyday basis is to plot the cycle of the moon, and to celebrate its various aspects in small ways during its passage through Dark to Full, and back again. Most people, whether working alone or in a group, will tend to have a 'circle' (explained later in this chapter) for at least one phase of the moon during the month. Very few will hold four 'moon circles' each month, unless particularly part of a personal, spiritual activity to link their own rhythms very closely with that of the Moon. In this chapter, there are examples

165

in the various exercises, of how one might celebrate these different phases.

This chapter will introduce you to ways in which you may like to decorate your home with Goddess-related symbols, create sacred space in your own home for specific occasions, create a 'Moon circle', and learn about the symbolism and power of different trees, flowers and herbs that you will find in your kitchen, garden or in the supermarket.

The Home

It is easy to create a space in which Goddess, element and other spiritual symbols are integrated. This is good news, especially if you share your living space with others, who may not necessarily be sympathetic to your beliefs! It isn't necessary to create a space that shouts 'Goddess freak!' with in-your-face statues, posters and drawings staring at you from every available shelf and wall-space. If anything, this might be a bit too 'busy' for most of us, who prefer to create a space of calm and comfort.

One thing you may wish to consider is the range of 'shapes' that influence your living space. You may find it easier to attune to the idea of spirals, circles and cycles if you live in a place where chairs are faced in towards each other, and other items of furniture form a circular shape around the room, instead of everything being 'square on'. Actually, this helps everyone, as you will be able to see each other when you are talking: it also enables people to observe body language as well as listen to the words that people are saying. Needless to say, improving one's intuitive powers — which are vital to magical and spiritual awareness — is vastly improved by being able to observe people's physical reactions during everyday conversations! Spirals and circles can be imported into the home scene without being too obvious — spiral-shaped mobiles are inexpensive and easy to make, and these can be hung in windows or gardens. Wreaths of dried flowers and decorated hoops can be hung on doors and walls.

Bringing the different elements into the house can be both straightforward and fun, too. You can use your creative talents in selecting pebbles, crystals and metals to represent earth, and glass, shells and water features indoors and out to represent water. Bringing fire into the home is now easier than it has ever been — even supermarkets now sell simple tin lanterns, candles and tea-lights. Air is catered for by making mobiles or dream-catchers with feather motives, and hanging wind-chimes or wind instruments at various divisions or junctures in your living space to symbolize flow and communication.

Colour is very important, for, as most interior designers and psychologists know, colour can affect both the atmosphere of a room and the state of mind of the people who frequent it. Integrating the associative colours of the elements, therefore, is a useful way of both creating 'spiritual space', and helping you to attune to their various meanings. The room I use to study and write in, for example, is a light yellow — the colour of Air, element of communication, concentration and clarity. Some people tend towards blues for the bathroom in any case, as a space that is a home to water. You might choose to pursue the water motif further by making your bathroom a space for de-stressing, and emphasize the symbols with which you decorate it as being of the element that brings healing and balance. These symbols might include mirrors, glass, shells, chalice-shapes — none of which are particularly outlandish to find in a bathroom in any case! Red, for fire, is a little more difficult, as one may not necessarily wish to have a bright red room, which in any case is liable to make people irritable and cross. Instead, you could bring bright red flowers or plants into an area where people tend to socialize. The colour red livens things up — just like its associated element, fire. Green, for earth, can be represented by having lots of green, leafy plants in your home.

Bringing Goddess symbols into the home is also very simple. There are lots of ways in which you can decorate your living space with typical Goddess symbols, such as snakes, dragons, spirals and circles. Decorations with specific Goddess symbols, those of Goddesses you have a particular affinity with, are also easily arranged. In my study, for example, I have at least two owl symbols, the totem of Athena, Goddess of wisdom — neither of which would stand out to someone who did not have knowledge of their significance.

Exercise: Making a Sacred Web Symbol

This exercise is really a 'how to' craft project — though one with a magical spin! If you wish to make something to place in your home that represents the interconnection that is such an important part of Goddess spirituality, the sacred web symbol is ideal. It is inexpensive, looks impressive when finished, and is a good way of bringing a little Goddess energy into your home.

For this exercise you will need:

- *One 15 cm diameter willow or other wooden hoop, available from a florist or craft store.*

- *4 metres of 0.5cm-width purple ribbon, to represent Spirit.*

1

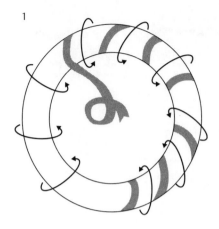

Wind ribbon around hoop
to decorate

2

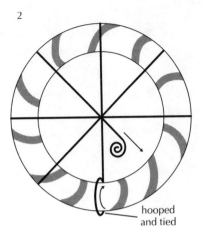

hooped
and tied

Using ribbon, secure 'spokes' to hoop
at the edges of the 'circle'.

3

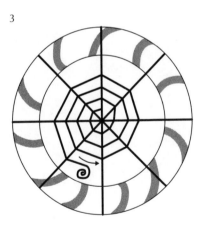

Begin at centre, fasten ribbon and weave
an outward spiral, looping the warp
around the spokes as you go

4

Fasten off your weaving then attach

Figure 3: Making a sacred wheel.

169

WAY of

- *1 metre each of 0.5cm-width yellow, red, blue and green ribbon to represent Air, Fire, Water and Earth.*

- *One pair of scissors.*

- *A hammer and a 2cm-long fine nail.*

1   *Loop and fasten the purple ribbon, at one end,*
     to the wooden hoop.

2   *Wind it at wide intervals around the hoop,*
     until you return to the original loop, and tie
     in a knot on the inside of the hoop.

3   *Stretch the purple ribbon across the hoop,*
     and tie off, forming a straight line across its
     centre.

4   *Loop the ribbon around the hoop and tie off*
     on the inside when you reach halfway
     between the two ends of the strand stretched
     across the circle, and stretch it across,
     forming a cross.

5   *Repeat the above process, so that there are*
     four strands pulled across the centre of the
     circle, dividing it into eight segments.

6   *Starting from the edge, and without severing*
     the ribbon, begin to weave a spiral around the
     circle with the ribbon, tying it off at each
     node to secure it, and ending at the centre. As
     you do, weave a little magic into your work
     by 'en-chanting' it with a Goddess chant,
     either one of your own making, or this:

     Comes the harvest, comes the seed,
     I am woven as I weave

7   *You should now have a web of purple ribbon stretched across the centre of the wood hoop.*

8   *Take the yellow, red, blue and green ribbons, representing the other four elements, and tie them in a bunch to the bottom of the hoop, trimming the ends to make them even.*

9   *Hammer the nail into a door or wall where you wish to hang your sacred web, and loop a little of the wound ribbon onto it to hang up your web. You now have an original and magical Goddess symbol to bless and decorate your home.*

The Work or Study Place

If you work outside of the home, it is likely that you will have a desk, work-station or office, or if you are a student, a common or home-room. Many of your colleagues may already bring in personal items, such as photographs of partners or children, or have plants in order to make the work space less impersonal. If this is the case, it should be relatively easy for you to bring your own personal items into your working or study space. You should remember, however, that work and study space is even more public space than if you share your home with others, and you will need to take account of work-place policy as well as the feelings of others. Having a three-foot high statue of Kali in your office, therefore, might not be acceptable. However, having a carved pebble, a pocket-sized figurine or particular plants on your desk as symbols of your spiritual path, will probably not attract any unwanted attention.

Putting flowers and plants in the office or home-room is a great way of integrating and reflecting your spiritual affinities into your work-aday life. There are a number of plants that are dedicated to different Goddesses, and you can find this out by doing a little research yourself. To help you in this, there is a short, indicative guide at the end of this chapter. However, you can find out a great deal by reading herbals, such as Culpepers, which is a 16th-century glossary incorporating a number of planetary associations. These herbals, alongside books and dictionaries of classical and ancient myths, are good guides to finding out which Goddesses various plants might traditionally, or even contemporarily, be associated with. For example, the olive tree is traditionally associated with Athena, as it is considered Her gift to Athens. Nowadays, miniature olive trees can be purchased from gardening stores, and brought into the work-place, if you are a great Athena fan. A herbal example is that of mugwort, otherwise known as artemesia — this is dedicated to Artemis. The rose, associated with love, is the flower of Aphrodite, the Iris (or 'flag') the flower of the Goddess of the rainbow, the daisy and dandelion with Brighid, and so forth. You can have a miniature tree, plant or spray of flowers in the office without many remarks being made, but the visual reminder, and scent of these plants, will keep aspects of your favourite Goddesses in mind to help you through the day. Many office workers and students have mascots or totems either tied to their rucksacks, or placed on their work-stations these days. Quartz crystals are a common sight in many offices, as are pot-pourri dishes. Having a pebble with a spiral carved or painted onto it, or a 'hagstone', that is, a stone with a hole worn through it naturally by the sea, is not something that will stand out, particularly. Similarly, a dish with pot-pourri scented with specific oils, such as lavender (for Air), patchouli (for Earth), geranium (for Water) or cinnamon (for Fire) should not attract any notice, either.

Having spiritual symbols about you can help make work territory a place you fit into more naturally, and this in turn can empower you in your working role, and reverberate powerfully within your spiritual development. It is important, however, not to get too intense or fetishistic about them, as this leads to superstition and anxiety, rather than spiritual development. Having meaningful items around you is an affirmation of your own spiritual development and empowerment, and you should be able to relax about this. It doesn't matter, therefore, if someone touches your things, or they get moved or lost — nothing dreadful is going to happen! They are simply shadows of your inner beliefs, which are there to reflect back the affirmative and celebratory nature of the way of the Goddess.

Protection Against Stress

Everyday life can be very stressful, and with stress-related sickness as a major cause of absence from work nowadays, it is important that we take care of ourselves! Hopefully, our home is a sanctuary from the stresses that impinge on us in the work or study place, but home, too, has its strains and anxieties from time to time. Making your home a restful and supportive place to be, both through actively improving and facilitating relationships within it, and ensuring, as far as possible, that our surroundings are nurturing and peaceful, is one way in which to fend off excessive stress. Personalizing our work or study space by integrating empowering and meaningful symbols is one way of making it more psychologically 'comfortable'. Another is to actively help build good working relationships in that space, and ensure that we are ourselves organized and up to speed on our work wherever possible and reasonable. However, there are times when excess stress seems unavoidable — for example, when you are working to a deadline and stress is attached to a particular task, or when a particular person, who is difficult to work with, induces anxiety in others. These are the times when you can invoke Goddess power in order to help you cope with the momentary panicky feelings.

One of the ways of drawing upon Goddess power is described in the exercise below. Others can be drawn from your knowledge of the associations of the elements, for example, visualizing yourself as breathing out anxiety (red/fire) and breathing in calmness and balance (blue/water). Your relationship to and knowledge of different Goddesses can be useful here, too: at times when you feel intimidated or threatened, you can visualize a particularly protective and fierce Goddess, such as Oya, standing behind you, hands on hips, or arms folded, ready to leap in and protect you! Better still, you can invoke Her power — that is to say, find the part of yourself that *is* Oya, and adapt Her courage and protection to your situation. Imagining yourself surrounded by a cocoon of bright, white light is also a good ploy when the walls are pressing in. Some people find it useful to have something physical they can touch or hold when they need to call up some psychic 'defence' at points of high anxiety — this is where pendants, pebbles or crystals can come in useful, as they are naturally tactile and comforting.

Needless to say, these tips and exercises are useful in themselves for coping with crisis moments, and for getting into the habit of becoming calm in the face of unwanted and unhelpful anxiety. However, if you continue to be anxious, you may need to ask yourself whether this is because of the situation you find yourself in, rather than your inability to cope. A boss or tutor who makes unreasonable demands may well be the cause of your stress — in which case, you will need to speak with someone in the human resources sector or your workplace, or seek advice from a union rep. Housemates and friends

WAY of

who stress you out with their problems, arguments or unwillingness to carry some of the responsibilities for the bills, arguments, housework, or for maintaining friendships may also be the cause of anxiety at home — and you will need to think about how to change this.

Exercise: Copper Shield Visualization

This exercise is intended to help you develop your visualization techniques, as well as provide a powerful method for fending off extreme stress. You can use this as often as you like — it doesn't keep the world away from you, and no harm can come from using it frequently. It just helps you to filter off the worst excesses of anxiety. Practise this at home first, so that when you find yourself at a point when you wish to invoke your Copper Shield, you can do so automatically.

1   *Slow your breathing.*

2   *Begin to take deep, slow breaths in through your nose, exhaling through your mouth. Do this for at least 30 heartbeats.*

3   *Continuing to breathe slowly and evenly, in through the nose, out through the mouth, allow your breathing to become slightly more shallow.*

4   *Continue breathing naturally, and visualize a beam of golden light emanating from your solar plexus.*

5   *As the light comes from the solar plexus, it begins to form a bright, oval shield, widest point upwards. This shield of light covers you from your throat to your knees.*

6   *When the shield is fully formed, it changes to a bright copper colour. You can visualize onto it any emblem that you choose — a Gorgon head, a dragon, a lion, bear or a striking cobra — anything you feel will defend you.*

7   *When you feel stress beginning to effect you, imagine the shield bouncing away any stress, harassment, or fear that is coming towards you.*

8   *This shield covers the sites where most people are vulnerable to stress — the bladder, the stomach, the chest and the throat — keep it there until the acute period of stress passes, then allow it to fade away naturally.*

9   *If you are having a particularly bad day, you can strengthen your Copper Shield in a moment by imagining more golden light coming from your solar plexus, and rebuilding it.*

10   *You can use this exercise as frequently as you wish — the copper shield is drawn from ancient traditions that associated copper and oval shapes with various Goddesses in the past.*

Making Sacred Space

At various times, especially when we wish to cast spells or take part in rituals, Goddess people make a sacred space where this can happen. Since very few of us have homes large enough to keep space aside especially for this purpose, we take the sacred into the everyday by holding these events in our living rooms or bedrooms. Once we have finished using these rooms for magical or ritual purposes, they are returned to their usual purpose.

There are a variety of ways in which people like to 'declare' or make their space sacred. Some people like to simply psychically purify an area by doing a salt and water blessing. This entails cleansing water, blessing salt, mixing the two together, and sprinkling it in a circle around a room to sweep out its usual function and replace it with a ritual function. The way that this is usually done is as follows. Pour a little spring water into a bowl or large shell, and concentrate on directing your will through the index finger of your writing hand. Point this finger into the water and concentrate on sending your energy through it to drive out any latent energies residing in the water. This clears the way for a blessing of salt. Then bless the salt, usually held in a bowl or seashell, by placing a hand on it, before pouring the salt into the water and saying a few words over it, eg: *'The water is pure, the salt is blessed, the space that it honours is space well dressed.'* At this point the salted water is sprinkled all around the room to clear the space and ready it for a ritual.

Another way of declaring and demarcating sacred space is by visualization. This requires visualizing a circle of light all around the room in which the ritual is to be held. The imagined circle is then spun around on its various axes to form a sphere of light that encompasses the whole room. This is a good way of preparing for a ritual, as it requires a level of stillness and meditation in order to visualize and mark out the space.

The most common way of making sacred space, however, is known as 'casting a circle'. This is the usual context in which we cast spells and perform rituals. Sometimes, we cast circles or create sacred space in order to sit and meditate, or go on inner journeys or meet with the Goddess, privately, in our own heads. This is because the circle is a space between the worlds, a place where we step into Goddess-consciousness in real-time.

Casting a circle is pretty straightforward. There are various ways of doing it, and no doubt once you are accustomed to creating your own sacred space, you will find other ways and settle upon your own preference. In the meantime, however, the exercise below gives you the basic framework of circle-casting — one that is most commonly used in the Goddess community.

Exercise: Casting a Circle

This exercise will set out a basic layout for casting a circle — or clearing, marking and claiming sacred space. This is basic to all spell-casting and ritual performance, and can be adapted to various purposes, including some of those described in the course of the next two chapters, which are about Goddess magic, and Goddess rituals. You are strongly advised to try casting a circle just to experience preparing sacred space, and being in it, before proceeding to build space for specific spells and rituals.

For this exercise you will need:

WAY of

- Either *five coloured candles to represent each of the five element colours — Yellow, Red, Blue, Green and Purple, or five tea-lights, each marked with the symbol of an element (those described in chapter four) by inscribing it in the wax surface with a needle point.*

- *Matches or a lighter.*

- *A space where you will be undisturbed for at least 30 minutes.*

  1   *First, place the tea-lights at equal points in the imaginary circle in which you will be working. Ensure that these are on heat-resistant surfaces or in proper holders. Place them in the order that they are usually placed around the five-pointed star; top point Spirit, top right, Air, bottom right, Fire, bottom left, Earth, top left, Water.*

  2   *When the candles are set out, go to the centre of your circle, with matches or lighter to hand, and concentrate on preparing yourself for a ritual. This requires that you are calm, so slow your breathing, and relax your body.*

  3   *Close your eyes and imagine yourself drawing in energies from below your feet, from the earth. Visualize this as green light rising from the ground, and travelling up through your body.*

4   *Then, as you draw in breath, visualize
     yourself drawing in energies from the air
     around you. Visualize this as yellow light.*

5   *Next, visualize yourself manifesting energy
     from the water in your body, in your blood.
     Visualize this as blue light.*

6   *Then, visualize yourself drawing energy from
     the light sources around you. Visualize this as
     red light.*

7   *As the colours blend together, they become
     purple, then white light.*

8   *Open your eyes and, beginning with the
     element of Air, walk around the room in a
     circle, staying inside the candles which mark
     the boundary of the sacred space you are
     creating. This walk around is to accustom you
     to the shape and boundary of the circle.*

9   *When you have circumnavigated the circle,
     come back to the Air candle. Facing outwards,
     and drawing the energy you have raised in
     your body through your solar plexus and
     down your writing arm, direct the white light
     through your index finger into the air around
     you, and walk around the room, drawing a
     circle in the air, until it is completed and you
     are back at Air again. This is known as
     'describing' a circle.*

181

10   *When the circle is completed, come back to
        the centre, and say:* This is the space
        between the worlds, a sacred space claimed
        for a sacred purpose.

11   *Now move to the element of Air and,
        saying:* Element of Air, bringer of clarity,
        communication and flow, you are honoured
        in this circle, *light the candle.*

12   *Moving on to the element of Fire, say:*
        Element of Fire, bringer of passion, courage
        and strength, you are honoured in this circle,
        and light the candle.

3   *Next, moving on to Earth, say:* Element
        of Earth, bringer of stability, wealth and
        manifestation, you are honoured in this
        circle, *and light the candle.*

14   *Moving on to Water, say:* Element of Water,
        bringer of healing, balance and love, you are
        honoured in this circle, *and light the candle.*

15   *Lastly, moving to Spirit, say:* Element of
        Spirit, bringer of connection, patterner and
        weaver, you are honoured in this circle, *and
        light the candle.*

16   *You are now in a sacred space, a circle marked
        out by your imaginative energies, and into
        which you have invoked, by honouring them,*

*the elements of all life. You may choose to
stay a while in the circle, seeing if you can
detect the different energies attached to the
elements, and meditating for a while.*

17   *When it is time for the circle to end, all you
need to do is visualize the circle widening outwards, beyond the room, beyond your house,
wider and wider until it fades away in space.
You can then blow out the candles, and use
them again at a later date for another circle.*

18   *Whenever you finish a circle, you should
eat and drink something in order to 'close
down' — just as you should when you
are doing visualization exercises. If you
walk around all the time in an extremely
aware and sensitive state, you will not be
able to defend yourself from other people's
stresses and bad vibes, and this will become
a problem. This is why, in communal circles,
we usually include some drink and food at
the end.*

This basic model for casting a circle will stand you in good stead,
even if, in future, you find your own personal way of marking out
and making sacred space. It provides a straightforward way of
declaring and marking out space, especially if you decide to work
with a group, or get a group of friends together to work ritual. It will
probably take a lot of repetition before you become accustomed to
the changes in energies within and around you during a circle, as
this only comes with practice. It is probably a good idea, therefore,

to keep to this basic framework to start with, and expand your repertoire, and wording, as you become more confident.

Celebrating the cycles of the Moon

Previous chapters have already mentioned the importance of the Moon in Goddess spirituality. Many groups meet at full moon to cast a circle, and do ritual, developmental and magical work together. Some groups like to vary this by sometimes meeting at different phases, such as Dark Moon, or the waxing or waning Half Moons. Individually, it is a good idea to mark these different moon phases with a circle, as they all have different associations and are suited to different purposes and types of spells. If you decide to join a group in future, you may find that established groups have their own traditions and ways of doing things. However, having practised alone and in a slightly different way is not a problem — rather, it is an advantage to have had some circle-work experience, especially with the moon cycle, which gauges different psychological and psychic periods.

Over the next four months, you might try celebrating different phases of the moon. These are described in more detail below, and are followed by a brief description of a suggested ritual. These are not meant to be prescriptive or definitive in any way — merely to offer you an opportunity to see how it can be done, and to provide a framework to build on in future.

The Waxing Moon

The waxing moon is a good time for doing spells for increase, attraction or moving forwards. This tradition comes from sympathetic magic, which connects intent with a symbol; in this case the symbol is the moon phase that reflects the intent of increase, bringing something towards you, or moving towards something.

The patron Goddess of this moon phase in its early stages is Artemis, whose bow is seen in the waxing crescent moon. From the Moon's first quarter, or the first Half Moon, its patron Goddesses vary from Innanna at Half Moon, to Astarte as the moon moves towards fullness. The symbol for this period of the moon is a crescent, horns pointing upwards.

Exercise: First Crescent Circle

This circle is specifically for the early waxing crescent phase. Circle structure below is flexible enough for you to build in activities of your own making.

1 *Cast a circle in the usual way.*

2 *When the circle is cast, invoke the elements in the following way, before lighting their respective candles:*

Element of Air, bring to this circle freshness and new ideas.

Element of Fire, bring to this circle the spark of creativity and new beginnings.

Element of Earth, bring to this circle fertility and new shoots.

Element of Water, bring to this circle cleansing and new birth.

Element of Spirit, bring to this circle magic and connection.

3   *Standing in the middle of the circle, when you have raised your own inner energies, read or speak aloud the following, which is a 'Goddess Charge', or expression of the Goddess spoken in Her words:*

Hear the words of Artemis, huntress and Goddess of integrity and self-reliance. I am She who roams wild in the forests of night, who dances with Her followers under the light of the Hunter's Moon. All those who call upon me are heard, and I give power and energy to those whose energy and love is directed to the poor, the disadvantaged, and the powerless. I am the Goddess of the night sky as the moon rises to full. I wear the horned moon on my brow, and breathe freshness and growth upon the Earth.

4   *When you have done so, light a white candle in the centre of the circle to honour Artemis.*

5   Sit down in the centre of the circle, and
    absorb the energies you have invoked through
    Artemis.

6   Think about the new things in your life, the
    things you wish to attract to you, or ways in
    which you need to move forwards. Write these
    down on separate pieces of paper, and speak
    them aloud before burning them over the
    white candle.

7   Place the ash of these words in a bowl, to be
    mixed with compost later. The compost in
    question should be used to grow a bulb, or
    seeds, in order to help your intentions grow
    and manifest in your everyday life.

8   Sit for a while in the peace of the circle, either
    meditating or speaking inwardly with
    Artemis, or chanting or singing something
    suitable for a first crescent circle, eg: Flow
    with the tide, Grow with the Moon, Turn
    with the Earth, Burn like the Sun.

9   When you are more experienced, you
    can include spells for increase, attraction or
    moving forwards at this point of the circle.

10 When you are ready to end the circle, thank
    Artemis in your own words for being present,
    visualize the circle widening out and fading,
    and extinguish the candles.

187

The Full Moon

The Full Moon is a good time for doing spells for healing, and basking in and showing gratitude for the good things in our lives. Most working groups hold group circles at this time, and the healing motif has become traditional mainly because of the many requests brought forward for healing at this time. The Full Moon is a time of prophetic and particularly meaningful dreams, and since the Moon is seen as the mirror of the soul, Full Moon circles are sometimes used for 'divination' or seeing patterns in one's life with tarot cards, rune stones or meditation on a particular symbol.

The patron Goddesses of the Full Moon phase include Astarte, Aphrodite, Selene and Demeter — all Goddesses of full-blooded sexuality or of fertility and parenthood. The symbol for this period of the Moon is a circular disc.

Exercise: Full Moon Circle

This circle is specifically for the Full Moon. The circle structure below is flexible enough for you to include your own activities as you grow more practised and confident.

1   *Cast a circle in the usual way.*

2   *Invoke the elements before lighting their respective candles, saying at the appropriate point:*

Element of Air, bring to this circle the power of clear seeing and clear thinking.

Element of Fire, bring to this circle the
power of strength and courage.

Element of Earth, bring to this circle the
power of manifestation.

Element of Water, bring to this circle the
power of dreams and psychic visions.

Element of Spirit, bring to this circle the
power of transformation.

3 *When the elements are invoked, stand in the
   centre of the circle, and read, or recite the
   following Goddess Charge for the Full Moon:*

These are the words of Aphrodite/Selene/[Full
Moon Goddess of your choice]. I am the
spirit of nature, I am growth, life, and love. In
my face are reflected your dreams and
desires, and I encompass all that was and will
be. All who celebrate the joys of life and love
do me homage by these actions. I am a cauldron of pleasure and plenty, and I rejoice in
life's good things. My very light heals the
spirit, and those who dance in that light
dance their way free from madness and
restriction. I am She who was with you from
the beginning of your life, and I am She who
will be with you at the end. But now I greet
you in the midst of life, and bid you live well,
love well, and be happy.

4   *When you have done so, light a white candle in the centre of the circle to honour the Goddess you have invoked.*

5   *Sit down in the centre of the circle, and absorb the energies you have invoked through Her.*

6   *Think about the things in your life that have come to fruition, the things you are thankful for, and the things you wish to change, or heal. Carve these a word at a time onto a round cake or biscuit, with a knife. Eat the cake or biscuit.*

7   *Do the same with a second cake or biscuit, to be left outdoors for the birds, when the circle is ended.*

8   *Sit for a while in the peace of the circle, either meditating or speaking inwardly with your Full Moon Goddess, or chanting or singing something suitable for a Full Moon circle, eg:*
I am a circle within a circle, With no beginning, and never ending.

9   *When you are more experienced, you can include spells for healing, and activities allied to divination of various types at this point of the circle. You may wish, if you are already competent in some of these, to do a tarot reading for yourself at this point.*

10   *When you are ready to end the circle, thank*
      your Full Moon Goddess in your own words
      for being present, visualize the circle widening
      out and fading, and extinguish the candles.

Waning Moon

The Waning Moon is a good time for doing spells for decrease, deflection or diminution. The Waning Moon is an ideal time in which to get rid of things we don't need, or remove ourselves or others from circumstances that are made difficult through our, or their, presence. This is the phase dedicated to cutting away the 'dead wood' in our lives, and for repelling those things that we need to keep away. It is a good time for shedding bad habits, and replacing them with good ones!

The patron Goddesses of the Waning Moon include the Morrigan, Sekhmet, the Cailleach and Hecate — all either fierce destroyers or midwives and guides through the terrain from life into death. The symbol for this period is the crescent Moon, horns pointing downwards, signifying the sickle that cuts downwards.

Exercise: Sickle Moon circle

This circle is specifically for the waning crescent Moon — sometimes described as the Sickle Moon. The circle structure below is flexible enough for you to include your own activities as you grow more practised and confident.

1   *Cast a circle in the usual way.*

2   *Invoke the elements before lighting their respective candles, saying at the appropriate point:*

Element of Air, summon your fresh breezes to sweep away and provide a path for change.

Element of Fire, summon your flames to burn away that which is no longer needed.

Element of Earth, summon falling leaves to bury things lost and forgotten.

Element of Water, summon your waves to sweep and wash away that which is past.

Element of Spirit, summon the Webster to weave new patterns.

3   *When the elements are invoked, stand in the centre of the circle, and read, or recite the following Goddess Charge for the Sickle Moon:*

These are the words of Sekhmet/Morrigan/Hecate/[Sickle Moon Goddess of your choice], Goddess of the Waning Moon, destroyer of that which is passing and no longer needed. In my face you see the sickle, instrument of cutting down and removing.

Yet in me all living beings find the mercy
and compassion of the end of pain and suffering. All those who dance in the light of
my beams are blessed with the wisdom to
let go of things they no longer need, or even
never truly possessed. To those I offer
knowledge and insight into the ways of the
world and the mysteries of life and death.

4   *When you have done so, light a white candle
     in the centre of the circle to honour the
     Goddess you have invoked.*

5   *Sit down in the centre of the circle, and
     absorb the energies you have invoked through
     Her.*

6   *Think about the things in your life that have
     come to an end, the things you wish to come
     to an end, and write them down on a sheet of
     paper. Fold the paper into halves, quarters,
     then eighths, and cut it into pieces with a pair
     of sharp scissors. These pieces should be
     buried in earth away from your home after
     the circle.*

7   *Sit for a while in the peace of the circle, either
     meditating or speaking inwardly with your
     Sickle Moon Goddess, or chanting or singing
     something suitable for a Sickle Moon, eg:* Fruit
     and grain, fruit and grain, All that falls shall
     rise again.

8   *When you are more experienced, you can
        include spells for decrease, repulsion and
        diminution, and activities allied to decreasing
        or shedding different aspects of your life at
        this point of the circle.*

9   *When you are ready to end the circle, thank
        the Sickle Moon Goddess in your own words
        for being present, visualize the circle widening
        out and fading, and extinguish the candles.*

New/Dark Moon

The New Moon is often referred to as Dark Moon — that is to say, it represents a phase of the moon that we cannot see in the sky, as the disc is completely in shadow. This is a good time for starting new projects, for strengthening your psychic abilities, and for performing spells that bind wrong-doers from continuing their harmful behaviour. The Dark Moon is a time for resting, and recharging our energies. It is also a good time for taking stock, and strengthening our intuitive powers.

The patron Goddesses of the Dark Moon include Lilith, Changing Woman and Grandmother Spider, all Goddesses of magic, mystery, deep creativity, knowledge and wisdom. The symbol for this period is the darkened disc.

Exercise: Dark Moon Circle

Now that you have seen three different circles associated with three different moon phases, and have had the associations of the Dark

Moon described for you, you should be able to construct a Dark Moon circle for yourself.

Using your notebook, and following the guidelines of the previous circle exercises and rituals, construct a Dark Moon circle. You may wish to place a sheet of paper over the section below, which provides a list of things you might wish to include.

Dark Moon Circle: Suggestions and Notes

1   *You might have included the following functions of the elements in your opening invocations to them:*

Air — knowledge
Fire — light in darkness
Earth — shield of protection
Water — deep psychic energies
Spirit — shape-shifting and transformation

2   *The charge of the Goddess of the Dark Moon might include elements of mystery, transformation, psychic and magical powers, and creativity.*

3   *If you have tried to find a chant for a Dark Moon circle, you might consider including references to the Dark Goddess, creativity, wisdom and empowerment.*

4   *Activities might include blessing new projects, binding wrongdoers and recharging your energies.*

The Goddess in the Garden

As mentioned earlier in the chapter, certain herbs, plants, trees and flowers have Goddess associations. Some of these are easily tracked down through research into herbals and encyclopaedias of myth and magic — others can be associated intuitively. An example of intuitive association is that of linking the yew to Hecate — the yew has a life-span of centuries, and is often found in old graveyards. Given Hecate's links with the night-time, old age, wisdom and the passage from life into death, the yew seemed a natural tree to symbolize Her. You might like to try this with your patron Goddess. It could be that She already has a herb, plant, flower or tree linked to her through custom and tradition. However, if not, you can summon your research and intuitive abilities to find a link between the Goddess and the appropriate plant.

Whether you have a garden, a yard or a windowbox, there is always a space for a plant that has Goddess associations. Herbs are easy to grow, and many of them already have Goddess associations, for example, Sage is associated, naturally enough, with Crone Goddesses, Rosemary with Sea Goddesses, Mugwort with Goddesses of Prophecy and the Moon, and so on. Flowers are seasonal, and it is easy to plan your garden, yard or windowbox to have Goddess-related symbols blooming through all seasons. If you do not have enough space for a tree in your garden, you could always make friends with one in a nearby park, or woodlands. Elder is a Crone tree, Oak a Sun Goddess tree, Sycamore for Goddesses of Air and intellect, Chestnut for Water Goddesses, and Birches for 'destroyers' such as fierce Sekhmet.

If you have space out of doors, you can even plan what is known as a 'power-garden'. This is a way of expressing your relationship to the Goddess and the elements of life. It allows you to be endlessly creative with the design of your garden, whilst providing you with a sacred space out of doors, where you can meditate, or simply sit in peace. Sometimes very little space is needed to create something quite special, as you will see by the exercise for an outdoor power-garden below. If you do not have space out of doors, it is possible to create a mini power-garden, in a bowl. This, too, is explored in an exercise below. If you decide not to create a power-garden in exactly the way suggested in these exercises, I hope that you are inspired enough to create something yourself.

Exercise: Making a Power-Garden Out of Doors

This exercise will offer an example of what can be done in an outdoors garden, in order to create a little Goddess-centred 'shrine' or power-garden. This is to help you express your own ideas about your spiritual path and your relationship to the elements, and the Goddess.

For this exercise, you will need:

- *A patch of soil or sand approximately half a metre in diameter.*

- *3 one-metre-high canes.*

- *One ball of green or brown hemp twine.*

- *One large terracotta or pottery bowl or rounded pot.*

- *Sufficient gravel or shingle to cover the surface area (up to half a metre diameter circle).*

- *A variety of stones, shells, feathers, small mirrors, plants, and a tea-light to go inside the bowl or pot.*

- *Wind chimes, either home-made or shop-bought, or a mirror or shell mobile.*

1   Bury the ends of the canes at equal points around a circular area set aside for the structure.

2   Lean the canes inwards, and bind them near the top with twine so that they form a triangular pyramid.

3   Using the twine, weave it between the three canes to make links between them, leaving out one section, which will be the front of the structure. Stop weaving the twine around the canes when it is about two thirds of the way down — this is for safety reasons, as you may wish to light candles on the ground below the structure.

4   Place the wind-chimes or mobile in the centre of the triangular pyramid, suspending it from the joined canes.

5   Place the bowl or pot on the ground directly in the centre of the structure, and place a tea-light inside.

6　　Decorate the ground within and around the
structure with natural gravel or shingle.

7　　Hang the feathers, stones, shells and small
mirrors on the twine that is woven between
the two sections at the rear of the structure.

8　　Decorate the ground area with various shapes
and sizes of stones, creating different levels
and depths, and place small plants either
directly in the soil or in pots placed between
or on the different levels of stones.

9　　At night, in dry weather, you can light the
candle in the bowl to honour the Goddess of
the Earth, and of all growing things. In
particular, you will be honouring the Goddess
of your Garden by celebrating your spiritual
path within it, in such a personal way.

Exercise: Making a power-garden indoors

This exercise has all of the objectives stated above for the outdoor
power-garden, but aims to achieve this on a much more modest
scale.

For this exercise you will need:

- *One shallow bowl (approximately 20 cm diameter).*

- *One small pack good-quality potting compost.*

- *One small, slow-growing plant such as a cactus or aloe.*

- *One palm-full of naturally-coloured gravel or shingle.*

- *Collection of small shells, glass pebbles, rose and clear quartz tumbled stones.*

- *Three extra-long matches.*

- *Short length of extra-thin twine.*

1   *Fill the bowl almost to the top with the good-quality potting compost — the high quality type usually includes minerals, which can be seen sparkling in the soil.*

2   *At the edge of the bowl, plant the cactus or aloe and sprinkle the gravel or shingle in front and to either side of it.*

3   *At the opposite edge of the bowl, plant the three matchsticks, heads down, in the compost, and tie the tops together with the twine, forming a miniature triangular pyramid.*

4   *Beginning at the centre, lay out your carefully chosen collection of tiny shells, glass pebbles and tumbled quartz stones in a spiral, until it has spun right out to the edge of the bowl. Whilst you are doing this, 'en-chant' your*

*power-garden by singing or chanting a
suitable refrain over it, such as:* Root and
leaf, seed and flower, spiral round and raise
the power.

5   *You now have your very own indoor
power-garden, which should be placed
somewhere prominent, where you can see
the representations of the Goddess and the
elements you have chosen to have around
you. It needs very little care apart from the
occasional watering of the chosen plant.*

6   *Your indoor power-garden can always be
altered or added to later, and it provides a
good place to bury smaller items or ashes
of paper burned for spells. In addition, it
provides an obvious space to display stones
and crystals that you may acquire from time
to time.*

Bringing your spiritual beliefs and practices unobtrusively into
your everyday life is easy — it just takes a little imagination and
sensitivity. If you are lucky enough to have a flat or home to
yourself, you can let your creative powers run riot in providing for
yourself, and your visitors, a comfortable, nurturing and spiritually-
affirming environment. As you can see by the suggestions and
exercises in this chapter, this need not be an expensive affair. On
the contrary — it is really an opportunity to explore your own
creative abilities and your relationship to the Goddess in a very
personal way.

The ability to create sacred space for occasions like Moon circles, magical spells and other rituals may take a little practice, but will stand you in good stead for when you wish to begin exploring different types of rituals. It is particularly pertinent to the next two chapters, in which you will be learning about rituals for different life events, and the principles and practices of Goddess magic.

EIGHT

GODDESS
Magic

Magic is an important part of the Goddess-centred Universe. It is the spirit of connection, the element of the web that, with a little re-weaving, helps things change. In Goddess magic, we call upon the energies of different Goddesses to help us cast spells, and to bless our endeavours. We also draw upon the power of the elements, which are part of the Goddess Herself, in order to raise energy and work magic for healing, protection, drawing love, prosperity and sending away harm.

The language of magic-making is extremely interesting; we speak of 'weaving', or 'casting' spells. This is also the language of craftwork, specifically creative work traditionally associated with women. In Goddess spirituality, we are the weavers and the web at the same time; and given the right circumstances, this is the case for all humans. We see all existence as a great web, and in magic, we re-pattern the web we are weaving, to obtain a specific outcome. In doing this, however, we must work with the web, and not try to weave *against* it. To do this would be to require the tides to flow backwards, the Earth to stop rotating, the Moon to stand still. Since none of these are possible, asking for miracles is pointless, and self-deluding. Magic works with nature, not against it, and in Goddess magic, we work with the natural tides of the Sun, Moon and Earth in order to create a brighter, more interesting pattern in our lives.

There are various systems of magic used by contemporary magi-cians, some of which depend upon the principle of 'polarity' or opposites. This often includes a polarity of gender, in which 'mas-culine' and 'feminine' are seen as complementary pairs, and around which is woven a strict and prescriptive regime about keeping these in balance. In Goddess magic, however, we regard true balance as coming from within and around us, and do not acknowledge these principles of 'masculine' and 'feminine' as being natural forces at all: they are in fact socially-derived categories, which we regard as serving only to keep sexism alive within the magical and spiritual systems that subscribe to them. Goddess magic deals in holism, separating out the elements only so that we can appreciate the different gifts that they bring, and hang our positive and creative symbolism on them! Frequent spellwork helps to reinforce our relationship with the Goddess, our understanding of the elements and our own spiritual development.

The system of the elements is very important in Goddess magic, and we use their associations in order to construct simple spells using straightforward symbols. There is an unwritten 'rule' in magic that 'simple is best'. Using the system of elements for straightforward symbolism, and invoking the powers of particular Goddesses, enables us to keep things straightforward enough to make sense, and yet subtle enough to be effective.

Principles of Magic and Spell-casting

The ethics of Goddess magic are very straightforward and sensible. Work with nature and the web, not against it. If you banish something, replace it. Don't do anything with magic that you would not be prepared to do with your bare hands, were that possible and feasible. Be creative and work within the spirit of affirmative living. Don't get superstitious — superstition is lazy thinking. Goddess magic, on the other hand, is for active thinkers, and doers: Goddess magic is based upon self- and other-empowerment, not fear.

The working principles of Goddess magic are similarly commonsensical. Work in a circle to enable you to enter Goddess-consciousness more easily, and to amplify and contain the power of the spell until you are ready to release it. Symbolize your intent, and the subject of your intent in as constructive and simple a way as possible. Raise energy, by chanting, dancing, concentrating and directing power, to create a link between a symbol and its subject. Act upon these symbols in a way that represents what you wish to happen. Keep the symbols in a safe place, until the thing you have requested has come to pass. Do not talk about, or 'bother' the spell in any way, as this dissipates the energy raised around it.

Using magic is very much a part of our spirituality, and does not stand outside of it in any way. The principles we employ are exactly the same for acts of magic as they are for other parts of our spiritual path; they acknowledge the web, honour the Goddess and celebrate our power-within. Goddess magicians are weavers and patterners, who insert a new pattern code into the web to complement and enrich it. Consequently, the results of our magical spells are of a part with this, and are sometimes experienced as gentle, and gradual changes rather than overnight u-turns. But natural or gradual is occasionally best, as changes that happen in this way are, as a rule, longer lasting. There are exceptions, however, and sometimes spells obtain remarkable and striking results. Occasionally this is highly desirable — especially if you are working to prevent a harm-doer continuing in their damaging behaviour. In such cases, bindings or banishings are best if they are immediately effective.

There are a number of magical terms associated with different types of spells that it would be useful to know. To 'bind' a wrong-doer is to restrict their actions and bind them by their own behaviour — the more they struggle to do harm, the more tightly they become entangled in their own harmful actions. Another principle is that of 'banishing', meaning ridding yourself or someone else or something, usually bad habits or bad behaviour. Since nature abhors a vacuum, it is always wise to replace that which is banished, so that other bad behaviour or habits don't have an opportunity to fill the spot that has just vacated! This replacement principle is necessary even when you are very angry with someone — even more so, really, as replacing harmful action with constructive or helpful behaviour is a blessing all round.

'Raising energy' means to charge your spell with energy, and empower it. This can be done in a number of ways — speaking aloud in the circle is powerful, as words, too, are symbols that represent our desires and intents within the realm of magic. Dancing, chanting, concentrating and directing energy through our bodies have already been mentioned — these are traditional in many systems of magic, and have a very long history. The word 'enchant' means literally to chant power into an object. Dancing deosil (clockwise) in a circle is a renowned method for raising energy for positive change, to attract or draw, or for increase. Dancing widdershins (anti-clockwise) is rarer, and is usually used to banish something. You have already been introduced, in the last chapter, to a method of drawing energy into your body and directing it through your finger, and solar plexus. Since all energy returns to its source — the web — you do not need to worry about your own, or the Earth's magical energies being depleted in this particular way. It really is a case of what goes around, comes around.

One of the most important things to remember is the phase of the Moon that is most suitable for your spell. The Golden Rule is: waxing Moon for increase and attraction, Full Moon for healing and empowerment, waning Moon for decrease and repulsion, Dark Moon for new projects and psychic protection. The links between the phases of the Moon have already been discussed in preceding chapters, and you can check back if you are in doubt as to which is best, when you come to put together your own spells.

Another element of sympathetic association used in spellwork is that of planetary associations and days of the week. Over time, the different planets have come to be associated with different principles. In Goddess magic, we can associate these with different Goddesses and different aspects of our lives. These associations are purely symbolic, unlike the use of moon phases, when the Earth's and our own energies are as important as factors in their choice as their more symbolic function as images of growth-attainment-decrease-regeneration. This is a very simple guide to the associations between planets, life-aspects and Goddesses — you are strongly advised to use your own intuition, and knowledge gained through individual research, and begin to map out your own interpretations in your notebook.

Correspondences for spells, rituals and Goddesses associated with each planet are listed at the end of each section: these can be expanded through meditation, experience and further study.

Mercury   Athena, Sarasvati, Helen and other Goddesses of communication, travel, learning. Matters of expediency, commerce, examinations, tests, career, learning, writing, communications, the internet, electronics, concentration, memory, sound. Correspondences include lavender flowers and essential oil, ash trees, mistletoe, and myrrh and benzoin incense.

Venus	Aphrodite, Astarte and Ishtar — and other Goddesses of love, affection, beauty and relationships. Matters of love, affection, friendship, beauty, decoration and adornment, arts, children, the home, co-operation, harmony, peace, sexuality, passion. Correspondences include roses, geranium essential oil, apple trees, and jasmine and rosemary wood incense.
Earth	Demeter, Gaia, Ceridwen, Persephone — and other Goddesses of greenery, fertility. Matters of material gain, prosperity, physical improvement, financial stability, shelter and other forms of necessary sustenance, growth, improvement. Correspondences include ferns, patchouli essential oil, yew trees, and juniper and cedarwood incense.
Moon	Selene, Artemis, Lilith — and other Moon Goddesses. Matters of emotional and mental wellbeing, psychic power, divination, prophecy, the menstrual cycle, female reproductive system and fertility, magical ability, disclosing secrets, fooling enemies. Correspondences include poppies, lilies, mugwort, peppermint essential oil, willow trees and comfrey root, raspberry leaf and betony incense.
Sun	Brighid, Amaterasu, Sol — and other Sun Goddesses. Matters of success, health, the good things in life, happiness, children and family, poetry, creativity, strength and courage, the will,

recognition, excellence. Correspondences include sunflowers, rosemary, bergamot essential oil, oak trees, and vanilla pod, frankincense and cinammon incense.

Mars

Oya, Morrigan, Taranis, Macha, Gorgon/Medusa, Kali — and other Goddesses who are fiercely protective. Matters of power, galvanizing action, protection and defence, progress, righteous anger, exertion, fending off harassment, libido, willpower, energy. Correspondences include thistles, cacti, basil, pine essential oil, pine and hawthorn trees, and bryony root, holly berry and gum mastic incense.

Jupiter

Juno, Iris, Fortuna, Macha, Rhiannon — and other Goddesses of Justice, Fortune and Generosity. Matters of justice, fairness, balance, expansion, generosity, good fortune, fame, support, kindness, joy, celebration, community, sharing, plenty. Correspondences include sage, aniseed essential oil, chestnut trees, and nutmeg, clove and almond oil incense.

Uranus

Nephthys, Hecate, Isis, Annis and other Goddesses renowned for magical knowledge. Matters of arcane knowledge, magic, divination, magical power, discovery. Correspondences include broom, camphor oil, bay trees, and camomile, clover and black copal incense.

Saturn | Hecate, Morrigan, Cailleach and other Goddesses of restriction and discipline. Matters of binding, restriction, diminishing, bringing discipline, revelation, slowing down, halting. Correspondences include ivy, asafoetida, cypress essential oil, birch and elder trees, and juniper, marjoram and saffron incense.

Neptune | Mare, Yemana, Grandmother Spider, Rhiannon, and other Goddesses of water and dreams. Matters of dreams, prophecy, sleep, symbols, messages, mystery, transformation, change, balance, the space between the worlds. Correspondences include hyacinth, starflower oil, hazel or rowan trees, and thyme, valerian and wormwood incense.

Pluto | Nemesis, Lilith, Hecate and other Goddesses of death, rebellion, and revelation. Matters of wisdom and revelation through initiation into the mysteries, arcane knowledge, pay-back, irrevocable change, time, alternative lifestyles and views, subversion, de-railing schemes, mortality, the ancestors, banishment. Correspondences include cuckoo-pint, belladonna, cyclamen essential oil, cypress trees, and snapdragon, thorn and gum mastic incense.

Magical Tools

Some people like to have tools kept aside especially for magical use. This is fine, as long as you know that this is more for psychological than strictly magical purposes. An old kitchen knife is as effective as a highly ornate dagger, and a piece of string as significant as a silken cord if your intentions and energy raised are appropriate. Of course, if it is important to the magician that her/his tools are used specifically for magic, this will have an effect, as for them, no other instruments will do.

Some Goddess-identified witches like to use an 'athame' (a-thay-mee), a ritual dagger to direct their energy through in casting a circle, or charging objects with power. Other people are just as happy using their index finger — the choice really is a very individual one. Similarly, some people like to have wands to direct energy — these are usually made from wood, though some are made from rods of crystal or metal. Again — these are not strictly necessary, but if they help to direct your concentration, then use one. Another tool used in the circle is a chalice or cauldron. These are sometimes used in spellwork to hold water, or, in the case of a cast-iron cauldron, to place a fire in which to immolate different items in the course of a spell. A pentagram, on a disc or platter made from stone, wood or metal is sometimes used to hold bread, or place magical objects, too. There are also a range of practical tools that are used in spellwork, including different-coloured candles, votives or tea-lights, cords or ribbons for fastening items and binding spells. These tend to be more ad hoc and relative to the spell being cast at any one time. This is with the exception of the element candles, placed around or within the circle, according to taste.

The main magical tools mentioned above, however, also have a representational function in the magical circle. The athame or knife represents the element of Fire, the wand, Air, the chalice or cauldron, Water, and the pentagram 'disc', Earth. Some people also like to have a cord with them in the circle, to represent Spirit. If having these in your circle helps you to create the sacred space needed for spellwork, then by all means make, or obtain, them as your magical work develops and progresses. But please be aware that they are not strictly *necessary* for successful spellwork.

The same goes for robes, or special clothes to be worn in the circle — if wearing these helps to create an atmosphere in which you can tap into the mysteries of magic, then by all means wear them. If you prefer to work naked, then that is fine, too. Again — neither is strictly necessary for effective spellwork.

A very practical item to have is a 'spellbox'. This is a place to keep objects used in spells until the spell is completed — ie the desired outcome is obtained. This can be anything from an ornate wooden box with a padlock, to a plastic ice-cream tub. What really matters is that it remains undisturbed.

Casting a Circle for Spellwork

For spellwork, you should cast a circle in the way described in chapter seven. There is a tradition that you should always move deosil (clockwise) inside a magical circle, but I have not found that this affects ritual or magical outcomes one way or another. However, if you are working within an established group, they may prefer to keep this as a rule for a variety of purposes, so remember to check with the people you are working with.

The timing of a circle is important — but should never over-rule urgent need. Magical circles are best carried out at or after sundown, as our magically creative psychological and psychic powers are more to the fore at this time.

The order in which things usually go in a magical circle are as follows, though please note that not all elements are included at all times:

- *Purifying the area with salt and water — if preferred.*

- *Casting a circle, declaring your space.*

- *Honouring the elements, then lighting a candle to bid them welcome.*

- *Statement of intent — ie This circle is dedicated to [Goddess] who is being invoked for the spell or I claim this space for magical work on behalf of [name of person being helped by spell], etc. Some of the spells in this chapter begin by invoking the powers, or honouring the Goddess who is the patron of the spell in question — this provides an acceptable substitute for an outright declaration.*

- *Naming of symbols.*

- *Charging symbols with power to link them to subject/object of spell.*

- *Enactment of desired outcome (actions representing what you wish to happen).*

- *Sealing — words to 'seal' the spell ie* Let it be so! *or the more favoured archaic:* So mote it be!

- *Closing of circle.*

- *Disposal/secretion of symbols until such time as the desired outcome is met.*

Calling on the Goddess in Spellwork

Drawing upon the energies or associative powers of a patron Goddess during the course of a spell is common in Goddess magic. Once you have discovered your own patron Goddess, and have practised recognizing different Goddess aspects within yourself, drawing upon the power of a particular Goddess for expediting a spell should be very straightforward. When you come to construct your own spells, you will be able to work out which Goddesses, or aspect of the Goddess, will be most suitable to the task in hand. The spells laid out in this section have already made the selection, but you can adjust this if you are happier working with a Goddess other than the one stated at the beginning of the spell.

The spells below already include symbols for each Goddess invoked, in order to focus the magician's mind on Her energies and associations. When you come to put together your own spells, you should remember to incorporate into the circle some visible symbol, whether an object, colour or totem, sacred to the particular Goddess you are calling upon.

All of the spells below are written as though for personal use. Needless to say, you are free to adapt them for use for other people, if you are happy that their motives are honest, and only if they request it.

Spell for Love: Astarte

This is a spell for when you are ready to let love come into your life. It does not focus on a particular person — indeed, no love magic should, as attempting to interfere with the freewill of another is a waste of energy, and allows you to fixate, improperly, on someone who does not return your interest. This spell is to invite love to come to you, and therefore focuses on your powers of attracting affection, and on the tides and cycles of life, in order to bring someone who is worthy of you.

This spell should be carried out on a Friday, day of the planet Venus, who represents love and romantic attraction. It should be carried out on a waxing moon — as near to first crescent as possible — as you are drawing love towards you.

You Will Need

- *One red rose.*

- *One wine glass.*

- *One small bottle of spring water.*

- *One pink candle for affection.*

- *One red candle for passion.*

- *One white candle for Astarte.*

- *Three drops of almond oil.*

- *One rose thorn, or an ordinary sewing needle, or dress pin.*

- *One empty screw-top bottle of at least 3 fl oz capacity, with lid.*

- *An rose or geranium incense stick, or loose myrrh and rose-petal incense sprinkled on a lit charcoal disc in a fire-proof holder.*

- *Element candles.*

The Circle

1   *Cast the circle in the usual way, and welcome the elements.*

2   *Light the incense.*

3   *Light the white candle at the centre, saying:*

I call on Astarte, Bright Evening Star,
Goddess of love and affection,
To light upon one who is worthy and kind
And send her/him in my direction.

4   *Take the thorn, needle or pin, and carve into the side of the red candle, a serpent rising towards the wick — this is one of Astarte's symbols. As you are carving, chant or sing the*

217

*following words to raise energy, all the while
visualizing a figure walking towards you from
a distance, down a long seashore:*

I summon in love, I call you to me,
The bee to the flower, the flower to the bee.

5   *Anoint the pink candle with the almond oil,
continuing the chant.*

6   *Light the pink candle, saying:* Bring me the
affection I wish for myself.

7   *Light the red candle, saying:* Bring me the
passion that I can return.

8   *Take the rose in your left hand, and peel the
petals off with your right, dropping them one
by one into the wine glass. As you place each
petal in the glass, name a characteristic that
you feel is important in a future lover, ie*
kindness, honesty, intelligence, fairness, etc.

9   *When all the petals are in the glass, pour the
spring water in until the glass is almost full
and stir the petals around with the index
finger of your writing hand, directing the
energy of the spell into the water, saying:*

*May all these blessings come to me,
As I will it, so mote it be!*

10   Drink half the water, pour the remainder, with rose petals, into the empty bottle, and fasten the lid.

11   Allow the white, pink and red candles to burn down completely in a safe place and under supervision.

12   Exactly one moon cycle after this spell is cast, pour the rose-water in the bottle over yourself in the bath. A new lover should appear in the space of three moons.

Spell for Protection: Oya

This spell is used for protection of all sorts, including protection against the unpleasantness of others, stress and anxiety, bad dreams or upset. It helps you to build a shield against adversity — this does not mean that bad things cannot happen, simply that you are better able to cope with them, and fend off bad vibes. Casting this spell often has the effect of keeping detractors and bullies at bay because of the strength that you take into yourself, and thus project in your everyday life. Those who lack confidence in their own abilities are advised to try this spell, and gather strength from Oya, who is a fierce and no-nonsense Goddess and a wonderful ally. It is also a good spell for those who are starting out on the magical path — as you become more sensitive, it can be easy to forget to 'shut down' and this leaves you vulnerable and prone to pick up on other's stress, anxiety, grief, etc. This spell for protection will provide you with an effective barrier against the tendency to take and be swamped by other people's problems.

This spell should be carried out on the day of the Dark Moon, whenever it falls, as this is a good time to strengthen your psychic protection.

You Will Need

- *One white candle — to represent the honesty of your intent.*

- *One black candle — for Oya, representing her ability to diminish harm.*

- *One red candle — for Oya, representing her strength.*

- *One salt shaker, containing salt.*

- *One small mirror.*

- *One small item of iron (a nail if necessary).*

- *One ordinary sewing needle, or dress pin.*

- *One small screw-top jar.*

- *A frankincense incense stick, or loose frankincense, cloves and black copal sprinkled on a lit charcoal disc in a fire-proof holder.*

- *Element candles.*

The Circle

1   *Cast the circle in the usual way, and welcome the elements.*

2   *Light the incense.*

3   *Light the white candle in the centre, saying:*

I honour my own integrity and honesty.

4   *Light the black candle in the centre, saying:*

I honour and call upon Oya,
Her power to diminish and turn back harm.

5   *Light the red candle in the centre, saying:*

I honour and call upon Oya,
Her strength and courage.

6   *Take the needle or pin, and carve into the side of the black candle a zig-zag of lightning — this is Oya's symbol. As you are carving, chant or sing the following words, or words you have written yourself that are appropriate to the spell, to raise energy:*

Oya thunders, Oya strikes,
Lend me strength and lend me might

7   *Continuing this chant, place the iron item or nail on the upturned mirror, and focus all your energies on it. This item represents your strength. See yourself, therefore, in miniature, seated on the mirror.*

8   Still chanting, take the salt shaker and pour a circle of salt around the iron item. This is your protection.

9   Continuing the chant, close your eyes and visualize yourself surrounded by a lightning-bright circle of protection, that you carry with you wherever you go.

10   When you are happy that you have taken on the symbolism seen in the iron item surrounded by the salt circle, cease chanting, and pour the item and the salt into the jar. Fasten this securely.

11   Allow the white, black and red candles to burn down completely in a safe place and under supervision.

12   At the first opportunity after the circle, bury the jar with the salt and iron item deep in soil, where it will be undisturbed.

13   You can strengthen your protective shield as frequently as you feel the need, every Dark Moon, if necessary, though you will not need the iron item, mirror and salt each time. Just use the candles, the chanting and the visualization to 'top up' your original spell, unless you move house, or your jar is disturbed, in which case repeat the entire spell.

Spell for Prosperity: Demeter

Spells for prosperity are spells for need — not *greed*. This spell for prosperity emphasizes material prosperity in the sense of those things that we require to be comfortable in our existence — the ability to provide ourselves with shelter, food, water, clothing, basic facilities, and pay the bills without anxiety. You need to be realistic about your expectations — this is a primary requirement of any spell for prosperity. You are not going to be rewarded with a bag of money on your doorstep, or a remarkable 'mistake' at the bank, which turns you into a millionaire. The underlying requirement for all spells for gain is that they are based on real need, and realistic expectations. If you are focussing on a specific thing that you need — ie a break from everyday life in the form of a holiday, or the ability to pay the bills, or to get necessary transport — this is generally very helpful. Vague requests tend to get vague results, so be explicit!

This spell should be carried out on a Monday — day of the Moon, and traditionally a day of money-related matters. It should be carried out on a waxing moon, as this spell asks for increase. Demeter, Goddess of Earth, fertility and material growth is an ideal patron for this spell.

You Will Need
- *One green candle — to honour Demeter, the element of Earth, and growth.*

- *One handkerchief.*

- *Three mint leaves.*

- *One small gold- or silver-coloured coin.*

- *A patchouli or sandalwood incense stick, or loose frankin-cense, myrrh, sandalwood or benzoin sprinkled on a lit char-coal disc in a fire-proof holder.*

- *Element candles.*

The Circle

1   *Cast the circle in the usual way, and welcome the elements.*

2   *Light the incense.*

3   *Light the green candle in the centre, saying:*

    I welcome Demeter, Goddess of Earth,
    Fruitfulness and plenty and
    Call upon Her blessing for
    [Your specific request].

4   *Lay the handkerchief out flat before you, and cup the mint leaves in both hands with the coin laid on top of them.*

5   *Concentrating on the leaves and the coin, which represent wealth and growth, visualize yourself in possession of the specific blessing you have asked for, looking happy. Whilst you are doing this, chant or sing the following, or any alternative appropriate words:*

Power of green and power of Earth
Grant me blessings of true worth.
Power of Earth and power of Air
Grant me all that's just and fair.

6   *Continue to chant throughout your*
    visualization, and when you are ready, place
    the coin and leaves in the handkerchief.
    Still chanting, tie the four corners of the
    handkerchief together, keeping the leaves and
    coin at the centre.

7   *Allow the green candle to burn down*
    completely in a safe place and under
    supervision. Place the handkerchief, mint
    leaves and coin in your spellbox, until the
    thing you have asked for comes to pass. When
    this happens, bury the leaves and coin below a
    willow tree, or weeping beech, to offer thanks
    to Demeter.

Spell for Healing and Balance: Rhiannon

Spells for healing should always take place on the understanding that you are working with, and not against nature. This means emphasizing balance and calm. A healing spell will not create miracle cures, but it may help the person concerned approach their treatment positively, and find a psychological equilibrium. This spell is a rather lovely way of seeking psychological, physical and spiritual balance in your life, and calls upon Rhiannon, Goddess of balance and resilience. Rhiannon is associated with the sea, and water is an element that has the remarkable ability to settle at its own level. It is also the element of healing, and love. This spell will help you to love and care for yourself, and find a healthy balance in your life. It is a gentle and powerful spell, which is highly beneficial if the person for whom it is intended takes part in it.

This spell should be carried out on a Sunday — day of the Sun, and traditionally a positive time for promoting health. You should carry out the spell on the waxing or Full Moon, as you are drawing healing towards you. The spell calls upon the powers of Neptune, the planet of water, dreams and psychic powers, and Rhiannon, Goddess of the waves and patron of balance and resilience in the face of adversity.

You Will Need:

- *One pale blue candle to honour Rhiannon.*

- *One deep blue or purple candle to represent Neptune.*

- *One needle or dress pin.*

- *One wine glass.*

- *One small bottle of spring water.*

- *Three clear or pearlized glass pebbles, representing respectively* mind, body *and* spirit.

- *Three accompanying tea-lights.*

- *A geranium incense stick, or loose frankincense, rosemary, and geranium petal or oil, and applewood sprinkled on a lit charcoal disc in a fire-proof holder.*

- *Element candles.*

The Circle

1   *Cast the circle in the usual way, and welcome the elements.*

2   *Light the incense.*

3   *Light the pale blue candle in the centre, saying:*

I honour Rhiannon, woman of the waves,
Goddess of justice and balance
Who embodies resolve, resilience,
Inner strength and peace.

4   *Light the dark blue or purple candle in honour of Neptune energy, saying:*

Neptune, planet of the mysteries of the
     waters,
Bring the healing and dreaming and balance
     for which you are famed
Into this circle where you are honoured.

5   *Using the needle or dress pin, inscribe in the side of this candle the sign of the trident, a symbol of Neptune and of water generally.*

WAY of

6   *Take the three tea-lights, and hold them in*
     your hands. Take one deep breath and breathe
     outwards onto them, saying afterwards: By
     my breath. *Then place them close to your*
     chest, saying: By my heartbeat. *Then cover*
     them completely with your hands, saying:

     By my hand,
     I bless and consecrate these candles as
         symbols of
     My Mind, my Body and my Spirit.

7   *Using the needle or dress pin, inscribe the*
     first tea-light, representing Mind, with an
     upward-pointing equilateral triangle,
     traversed halfway down by a horizontal
     line. Then inscribe the second, representing
     Body, with a downward-pointing equilateral
     triangle. Inscribe the third, representing
     Spirit, with a five-pointed star.

8   *Place all three in holders or in a fireproof*
     dish, and light them.

9   *Pour the spring water into the wine glass.*

10   *Take the three glass pebbles, one at a time,*
     and begin to chant or sing the following,
     which is a popular chant for healing spells:

     Earth my body, Water my blood,
     Air my breath and Fire my spirit.

11   *Continuing the chant, place each of the*
pebbles in turn into the water in the glass,
visualizing yourself as calm, healthy and
serene, respectively.

12   *Still chanting, place the glass by a window, if*
possible, in the moonlight.

13   *Allow the candles to burn down completely, in*
a safe place and under supervision.

14   *After the circle, if the glass is not in*
moonlight, carry it outside under the stars for
a while, before returning it to a safe place,
where it should stand until the first day after
Full Moon. Then you can pour the water onto
soil where something is growing, and place
the three glass pebbles in your spellbox for
safe-keeping.

Spell for Work, Promotion or Success in Exams: Athena

This spell is a communication spell, and is suitable for seeking success in finding work, obtaining promotion, promoting success in interviews, exams or tests. It works on your communication powers, and the ability of others to appreciate what you have to offer. As you might guess, it will not guarantee results where a person is not prepared or qualified for the job, promotion for which they are applying, or the exam they are sitting. But it does offer you an 'edge' where good communication is necessary. Athena, Goddess of wisdom and learning, is also a Goddess of communication at all levels. As a weaving deity, as well as a patron of the intellect, she joins together ideas with their ensuing actions, and thoughts with their most appropriate expression.

This spell should be carried out on a Wednesday, day of Mercury the planet of communication. You should carry out the spell on the waxing Moon, as you are drawing success towards you. This spell works with Air, the element of communication, Mercury, the planet of speed and connection, and Athena, Goddess of all three.

You Will Need

- *Three yellow candles, one each for Athena, Air and Mercury.*

- *One needle or dress pin.*

- *Approximately nine drops lavender oil.*

- *A pine incense stick, or loose frankincense, pinewood and benzoin gum or oil sprinkled on a lit charcoal disc in a fire-proof holder.*

- *Element candles.*

The Circle

1   *Cast the circle in the usual way, and welcome the elements.*

2   *Light the incense.*

3   Take the needle or dress pin, and inscribe into
     the side of the first yellow candle, the symbol
     for Air, which is an upward-pointing
     equilateral triangle scored halfway through
     with a horizontal line.

4.   Inscribe the second yellow candle with the
     symbol for Mercury, which is a circle topped
     with a pair of horns, or upward pointing
     crescent, and tailed with a cross.

5   Inscribe the third yellow candle with the
     symbol for Athena, which is an upward-
     pointing equilateral triangle.

6   Take the candles in turn, and anoint them
     along their full length with the lavender oil.
     Set them in secure holders.

7   Light the first, saying:

     Element of Air, which surrounds and
          connects everything together,
     Bring your powers of clarity and
          communication to this circle.

8   Light the second, saying:

     Mercury, planet of teaching and learning,
          commerce and education,
     Bring your powers of speed of thought and
          quickness of tongue and pen to this circle.

9 *Light the third, saying:*

Athena, Goddess of wisdom, and learning,
Seen in the bright stars that fall from sky
    to earth,
Connecting thought with action,
Bring to this circle your powers of intelligence,
    quickness and all their expressions.

10 *Hold out your hands, palms upwards, in the
traditional position of supplication, and say:*

Power of three, sacred to communication
    and connection,
Bless me in my request for [your request
    for success].
So mote it be!

11 *Circle three times around the candles, singing
or chanting the following popular lines for
communications spells:*

Wearing my long tail feathers as I fly
Wearing my long tail feathers as I fly
I circle around, circle around the
    boundaries of the Earth.

12 *Continue chanting until you feel you have
raised enough energy, then close the circle.*

13 *Allow the candles to burn down completely, in
a safe place and under supervision.*

Spell to Diminish Harm: Sekhmet

Sekhmet is a particularly apt deity for this spell to diminish harm, as She is sometimes known as 'the Destroyer'. She slashes and burns away that which is not needed, effectively and finally, and so is ideal to call upon in cases where bad behaviour or habits are causing harm to yourself or others. The spell below is constructed for driving away harm caused by another person, but is perfectly adaptable for personal habits that you wish to be rid of. It should be emphasized that this spell is not a 'curse' of any kind; Goddess magic works affirmatively in that it concentrates on promoting what is useful and balanced. Getting rid of something that is causing harm or imbalance is perfectly in keeping with this philosophy.

This spell should be carried out on a Saturday, day of Saturn, the planet of restriction. You should carry out the spell on the waning Moon, as near to Dark Moon as possible, as you are working to diminish harm.

You Will Need

- *One black candle for Saturn.*

- *One red candle for Sekhmet.*

- *A 40 cm length of black cord.*

- *A frankincense or cinnamon incense stick, or loose frankincense, mugwort and cypress leaves or oil sprinkled on a lit charcoal disc in a fire-proof holder.*

- *Element candles.*

The Circle

1   *Cast the circle in the usual way, and welcome the elements.*

2   *Light the incense.*

3   *Light the black candle, saying:*

I invoke the powers of Saturn, planet of
    restriction and discipline,
To aid me in my spell to drive away the
    harmful behaviour of [name].

4   *Light the red candle, saying:*

I invoke the Lady Sekhmet, the lion-headed,
    the Destroyer of harm:
Awake and drive out the harm caused by
    [name],
That they be freed from it, and all hurt from
    it ceases.

5   *Take the cord and hold it up before both candles, saying:*

By this cord I bind,
With this cord I wind
The harm of the doer,
By his/her harm entwined.

6   *Beginning at one end, and working your way along the cord at equal intervals, tie nine*

knots, reciting at each knot the appropriate line:

By rule of one, the harm is done
By rule of two, it rebounds on you
By rule of three, let no harm be
By rule of four, do harm no more
By rule of five, return to life
By rule of six, I have you fixed
By rule of eight, no hurt create
By rule of nine, you are entwined.

7   *Wind the cord into a tight ball, and fasten it.*

8   *Holding the ball in your hand, speak as if to the person whose harmful behaviour you are diminishing, saying:*

As by your own harm you are bound
All hurt inflicted will rebound
But if however you will cease
The good you do will thus increase.

9   *Since you are banishing a trait of bad behaviour, you will need to replace it with something positive, to prevent other types of bad behaviour replacing what you have banished. Think of something appropriate and, turning the ball upside down, say:*

Here is the blessing I will send
To s/he whose bad behaviour ends;

[name an appropriate blessing, ie kindness, understanding, respect for others etc.]

10   *Allow the candles to burn down completely in a safe place and under supervision.*

11   *Keep the cord in a ball in a safe place, then when what you have asked for comes to pass, bury it deep in earth where it will not be disturbed.*

Exercise: Making your own spells

Taking your lead from the spells offered within this chapter, your knowledge of the Goddesses, and of the elemental symbols and planets, try to construct a spell for yourself. You should consult the sections above on **Casting a Circle for Spellwork** and **Calling on the Goddess in Spellwork** to help you plan the order in which you place different actions, and to help you decide which Goddess or Goddess energy to invoke. You should re-read this chapter, paying particular attention to the section on Principles, to remind yourself about the ethics and principles involved in putting spells together. You may also find it helpful to consult earlier chapters, where Goddess and element symbols were discussed.

Here is a list of questions that will help you to plan a spell — you should ask these of yourself whenever you are planning to do some spellwork:

- *Is this spell really needed — have other, sensible ways of achieving the objectives already been tried?*

- *Is this request realistic?*

- *If you are doing spellwork for someone else, do they understand that results are not instantaneous or miraculous?*

- *Which Goddess/elements/planets are suitable for this spell?*

- *What timing is ideal, ie Moon-phase, day of the week (if applicable)?*

- *What can I use to symbolize what I wish to represent, and what I wish to happen to it/them?*

- *What words might I use to invoke/raise power?*

- *Is this spell as simple as it can be?*

- *What happens to the ingredients after the spell?*

Once you have answered these satisfactorily, you are ready to go — good luck!

GODDESS
Rituals

The use of ritual in Goddess spirituality is an extension of what is a natural, intuitive and common part of our everyday lives. All of us to some extent have taken part in rituals or ritualistic behaviour, even though we are not always aware that that is what it is. Lighting the candles on a birthday cake, decorating a Christmas tree, or having a Thanksgiving meal, with its familiar contents, are all forms of the more marked rituals in which we participate. Some rituals are specific to families, rather than the surrounding culture, for example, the time of day that you open presents on your birthday or a day of the week when all the family eats together. Less marked rituals also punctuate our everyday existence — such as doing the crossword *after* rather than *before* dinner, keeping Friday night as a night out with friends and Saturdays for your partner, or making a point of always having popcorn when the family watches a video together. Rituals, then, are familiar to us even if we are not accustomed to naming them as such.

The term 'ritual' as we use it in everyday language has come to have a number of meanings. It can sometimes be used to denote that which is habitual, repetitive or formal, ie *'She dreaded the ritual humiliation of the Friday afternoon sales count'*, or *'Outside of the building they offered each other cigarettes, the universal ritual of solidarity amongst smokers.'* In Goddess spirituality, it is used in its older sense, to refer to a symbolic enactment of what is being honoured or celebrated, within sacred space. In Goddess spirituality, rituals are taken a step further than those in which we participate in everyday life, and on public or family occasions, though some elements of these are incorporated. One of these is the use of symbols. Just as, at Christmas, we bring mistletoe into our homes for decoration, and for its charming tradition of kissing underneath it, in planned rituals, we use symbols that represent different aspects of the life-changes and celebrations we are marking. One of the main differences, of course, is that the symbolism we use in Goddess spirituality is slightly less well-known than that employed in a festival as widely celebrated as Christmas. Depending on the context of a symbol's use in ritual, it may well have a long tradition, but one that has fallen into disuse. Alternatively, it may be a symbol that we ourselves have chosen to represent something in the ritual space — and in the joyfully creative and inventive path that is Goddess spirituality, this is equally as likely!

In chapter seven, you were introduced to the concept of making sacred space, and shown how to cast a circle. In chapter eight, you were introduced to one of the main purposes of circle-casting; spellwork. The other main purpose of circle-casting in Goddess spirituality is to make a special space in which to create and perform a ritual.

The circles to which you were introduced in chapter seven are, in fact, rituals to honour different phases of the Moon. The rituals outlined in this chapter are mainly rituals to either mark, celebrate or instigate life changes.

All rituals within Goddess spirituality can be divided roughly into four sections, according to purpose. The first category contains those rituals that are to mark important times in our passage through the life-cycle. These, generally speaking, come after or during the event being marked, such as birth, puberty, parenthood, elderhood, or death. The second category contains those rituals that mark other types of life events, often instigated by cultural, social or personal events that are not necessarily tied into the biological life-cycle. These might include marriage or handfasting, divorce or partings, geographical relocation, achievements, or new beginnings. The third are rituals that are to cause or instigate change, such as 'initiation' rituals, where you are calling down spiritual energy to help you grow as you enter your chosen spiritual path, grieving rituals aimed at healing or understanding the processes of loss, and other rituals that help people to 'name' or mark an event, for example, one of violence or abuse to make it more 'real' and thus grow towards dealing with or making decisions about it. The fourth is to celebrate nature cycles such as the phases of the moon, or the eight festivals of the year. Into this category also fall those rituals that are regular events, such as group or 'circle' meetings, usually timed for different Moon phases.

In this chapter, we will be concentrating mainly on the first and second categories. This is because the third category is usually so much a personal decision that you will need to plan, or help someone else plan such rituals for themselves — and this chapter will give you the framework of ritual, and hopefully, inspiration for ritual work which you can adapt to this purpose. In the case of the fourth category, you have already been introduced to Moon phase circles, and the various purposes and features of the different festivals, which you should, following this chapter, be able to celebrate in ritual form.

Celebrating the Life-cycle

Our biological life-cycle creates certain notable events in our existence. Depending upon the cultural and social background we come from, some of these are marked already — for example, the arrival of a newborn is usually the cause of some celebration, be it a party or a 'naming' ceremony of some sort, such as baptism or presentation into the parents' religion. Other important biological events, however, are deliberately kept quiet, such as *menarche* or a young woman's first menstrual bleeding. Which events are marked, and which hushed up are the result of social preferences and pressures. The freedom to choose which major biological life-event you wish to mark, however, signifies a break away from such pressures and provides the possibility of choosing what you wish to mark, and how you would like to mark it. It also offers us the chance to choose what we wish to make significant, and the opportunity to value the passage of our lives differently. This is particularly important in a life-affirming spirituality such as ours. The social tendency to under-play and even keep hushed up, the fact that women menstruate at a certain time, for a certain time, and over a number of years, implies that this is somehow a 'dirty' secret. The chance to celebrate this turns the idea of 'shame' and 'abnormality' on its head, and offers young women — and their parents and friends — a chance to positively celebrate an important, wonderful and natural life event. By the same token, the process of ageing can be celebrated, instead of being feared, dreaded and even despised, by making it a cause for celebration at a 'croning' or 'elderhood' ritual or party.

There are other life events, not necessarily biologically based, many of which are a reason to celebrate, such as marriage, graduation, changing career, and some of which are less causes for celebration than they are a reason to pause for thought. The latter might include the break-up of a relationship, which may for some of us be life-changing. On the whole, although the pain of break-up is recognized by close friends, it is usually dismissed in the wider social web as 'something to get over' — the sooner the better. Ritual can provide a more helpful way of acknowledging this type of grief, and actual-ly help move it along in a healthier way than trying to forget about it. It is also possible to create rituals that mark new beginnings or endings that, like the ending of relationships, do not have a space in current social frameworks — or on the shelf in card-shops. These can be intensely personal, or social changes in our lives, and range from making a decision to quit an addiction to emigrating and starting a new life elsewhere. Either way, a person making ritual space for these events is assured of marking and eliciting change in a powerful way — especially if the ritual is shared with other people.

It is important that we are able to choose what we think is important in our lives, and to be able to register these changes in some way. Ritual works in much the same way as magic does — it creates a new pattern in the rich and splendid webs that are our lives. Ritual is not an empty symbolic gesture to signal to everyone else that something is happening, although of course it can function to signal to communities of family and friends that something has: it is itself a powerful and empowering way of signalling to the web that there has been an alteration. This reverberates within us, as well as outside of us, along the strands of the wonderful web that we call magic.

Men, Women, Life-cycles and Roles

In patriarchal society, men and women have different roles and functions that are culturally and socially sanctioned. This is true to such an extent that we even interpret our biological life-cycles through our social beliefs. Women, for example, are said to have entered elderhood at menopause, which is a biological event recognized socially. There are, to be sure, certain negatives associated with this within society, some of which are frankly sexist. However, there is a recognition that through the biological event of the cessation of monthly menstrual bleeding, women have entered another life-cycle 'zone'. For men, such an event does not exist, at least in social terms — and allegedly in biological terms.

But men do age, and experience ageing as surely as women do. It is the emphasis on the lack of reproductive function that renders this ageing more socially 'visible' in women than in men. And yet … considered differently, this need not be the case. Why the emphasis on reproduction when the majority of us do not produce more than two or three children within one lifetime? And why assume that the menopause is something that happens suddenly when, for many women, it is a process, like that of ageing in men, that takes a number of years? Also, the menopause is seen as unhealthy or as a crisis in women, as though it were not part of a natural process of ageing that we all encounter at some point in our lives, if we live beyond a certain number of years on the planet. If we start to ask questions about the way in which our life-cycles are understood in society, we can start to question the way that men and women are 'gendered', separated and treated differently to the detriment of women, first, and ultimately, both. Elderhood, for example, can be celebrated positively by both men and women, if we value it differently. And if we celebrate and mark it positively, it will come to have more positive connotations within ourselves, as well as in the wider social sphere. Our actions impact throughout the web, remember!

Celebrating different aspects of our lives, and valuing those aspects of them that have, for some reason or another, been devalued in our cultures, is really quite subversive in its own way. It effectively challenges us to see our lives differently, and to provide alternative ceremonies for those aspects of our lives that *have* been celebrated within society in some way. These might include looking at marriage ceremonies, which mark a certain type of relationship between men, women and families as they presently stand, and providing an alternative, where couples (and this includes same-sex couples) can choose what their coming-together marks. In this way, the true nature of their partnership can be celebrated, rather than have the nature of that relationship imposed by the State, or by social or cultural custom. Creating rituals for life-changes and our changing roles in our families, in society, is a positive way of creating wider change within and around us.

Exercise: Thinking About Rites of Passage

Section A
The term 'rites of passage' refers to rituals associated with our path through life. Using your notebook, and looking back over the introduction to this chapter if you need to, note down as many life-events that could be marked by ritual as you can think of. You may wish to cover up the suggestions in Section B below so that you can focus on thinking this through for yourself.

Section B
Some life-events that can be marked by a ceremony or ritual are listed in this chapter. These include: naming newborns, parenthood, handfasting (marriage), funeral and memorials, puberty, and elderhood. You may also have included some from the following list, which is indicative, and not definitive. If you have noted down some that do not appear here, they may well be valid life-changes to mark in ritual — think it through and decide, in the light of the following suggestions:

Divorce	Bereavement
End of relationship	Success in career
Career change	Grandparenthood
Recovery	New job
End of dependency	New home
Period of celibacy	Life-style change
'Coming out'	Exam success
Important journeys	Reconciliation

Revelation	Adopting a child
Moving out	Retirement from paid work
Reunions	Anniversaries of events
Inviting change	Changing your name
Gender reassignment	Making important resolutions

These are simply possibilities: what is important is that the person concerned deems the life-event important enough to mark with a ritual. It should be understood that all of these suggestions imply the *choice* to celebrate, rather than the absolute *necessity* to. There is, after all, no point in over-ritualizing everything that happens in your life, just for the sake of it. It is perfectly normal to proceed through a variety of these events without ever feeling the need to perform a ritual. If you do, however, there are lots of possibilities and ways of making this possible.

Welcoming Babies and Celebrating Birth

In Goddess spirituality, the birth of a wanted child is recognized as a cause for celebration. It is a very special event, especially for the parent/s. For a woman, giving birth can be many things, including traumatic, but it marks a departure from the old life, when you were without the baby, or when the baby and you were together in the same body. For a man, attending the birth of a child can be a moment of intense bonding between you and your partner, and the new little person you have helped create. In addition to the birth itself, there is a new person in the world, and given the energy that is usually expended in deciding upon a name, it is safe to claim that naming and welcoming the newborn is an important part of a baby's arrival, too.

Both the parenting and naming aspects of welcoming a newborn can be celebrated in ritual; though in the first case, the emphasis is on the experience of the parent, and in the second, the emphasis is on the naming and welcoming of the child.

Presently, unless you have a particular religion, there are no public rituals to mark the arrival of a baby. There is, however, often pressure from relatives, however removed they are from practising their religion on a daily basis, to mark the birth of a child with a religious ceremony, for example, baptism. In the absence of anything else, some couples give in, for the sake of having a celebration that, even if it flies in the face of their own beliefs, provides a format for marking the newborn's arrival. In fact, there are many alternatives, the majority of which can be shared with friends and relatives.

One way to make a naming ritual more accessible to friends and relatives who do not share your beliefs is to throw a 'Naming Party' — a naming ritual constructed by yourself/ves, for your baby, and 'wrapped up' in a celebratory occasion. It would be a good idea to have a special cake, with the new baby's name on it, and some bright decorations that include candles, to symbolize the lights on the path you provide for your child. If you have some sympathetic friends, you can include them in a short ceremonial to name your baby, for example as 'Officers' at the different elements, bringing the gift of that particular element to the newborn. The Naming Ritual set out below offers some pointers on ways in which you could put together the actual ceremonial part of the event. The ritual below is set out to include five elemental Officers and two parents, though it can, of course, be performed by one parent, performing the ritual in private with just the baby, or with a couple of friends sharing the Officer roles between them.

WAY of

Naming Ritual for a New Baby

Prior to the ceremony, you will need to prepare by finding out about the meaning of the name you have chosen for your baby, and also which family members or people you admire who have shared this name. You should also ask your guests to prepare by thinking of something they would want to wish the baby to help her/him on her/his way in life, for example 'the ability to make friends', 'patience', 'kindness', etc. You should also fix on a Goddess to watch over the baby as s/he grows, so that you can name Her as the baby's sponsor in her/his early years in the course of the ceremony. You will also need, before the ceremony, to identify certain people to carry out other tasks, such as the coin-pressing, the offering of the chalice and the blowing of bubbles. Each parent should prepare by either writing down what you wish for your child, or selecting an appropriate poem or tract to read out. It would be a nice touch to have a friend playing an acoustic instrument gently in the background as the guests move forward to speak their wishes and light their candles. As ever, the Element candles should be positioned at equidistant points around the circle.

You Will Need

Personnel

Baby, Mother and Father

One Officer each for Air, Fire, Water
Earth and Spirit (could be dressed in
the associated colours for a
colourful ceremony!)

Ingredients

Element candles

A geranium or jasmine-
scented incense stick

Grandparents and other relatives
and friends

Three tall white candles

One tea-light for every
guest
A chalice or wine glass
A thimble of salt
A coin
A bottle of bubble-blowing
liquid
A small bottle of spring
water
Circlet of flowers for
baby's head

The Ritual

1   *The Element Officer for Air opens by
declaring sacred space, and walking around
the room or the garden whilst saying the
following words:*

As I walk this circle round,
I create it as sacred ground,
Blessed by those who gather here,
Warmed by wishes and good cheer!

2   *The incense should be lit.*

3   *The Element Officer for Air should then read
or recite aloud the blessing for Air, which
is directed to the baby, before lighting the
appropriate element candle:*

The blessings of Air are intelligence, the ability to learn and to communicate. May you obtain all of these as you grow.

4   *The Element Officer for Fire should do the same, saying:*

The blessings of Fire are courage, strength and laughter. May you prosper from these gifts as you grow.

5   *The Element Officer for Water should do the same, saying:*

The blessings of Water are love, balance and healing. May you embody all of these as you grow.

6   *The Element Officer for Earth should do the same, saying:*

The blessings of Earth are physical health, prosperity and stability. May you experience all of these as you grow.

7   *The Element Officer for Spirit should do the same, saying:*

The blessings of Spirit are connection, empowerment and transformation. May you bring all of these to the world as you grow.

8   *One of the parents should then say:*

We are here to welcome our new baby into
the community of family and friends, and to
give her/him a name.

9   *The other parent should say:*

We ask all of our family and friends to join
with us in offering your wishes for our
baby's future, with your declarations and the
lighting of candles.

10   *The parents should then say together:*

We name you [Name], a name that you
share with [...], who [...].

One parent continues: You are, however, our
[Name], a new person, and we wish for you
the right to develop as an individual, on the
shoulders, not in the shadow of those who
came before. *Other parent:* We bless you,
therefore, in the name of [chosen Goddess],
upon whom we call to bless and watch over
you as you grow, and ensure, with us, that
you are enabled to grow as a whole person.
*Place the circlet of flowers on the baby's head
and light the central tall white candle in the
centre of the ritual area.*

11   *The baby's grandparents, or some friends,*
should then present the chalice or glass, and
fill it with the spring water, saying:

May you never thirst in all of the days of
your life.

12   *Another should then press the coin into the*
baby's palm, saying:

May you never want or hunger in all the
days of your life.

13   *Another should then pour salt on the baby's*
other palm, saying:

May you never forget what is most important in all the days of your life.

14   *Another, whilst another two or more people,*
perhaps children, are blowing bubbles, should
say:

May you always witness and perceive beauty
in all the days of your life.

15   *The parents should then announce what they*
wish for their baby, either read out from a
sheet, or recited by memory, and afterwards
light each of the remaining two tall white
candles in the centre of the ritual area.

16   *Family and friends should then be invited to*
      come forward one by one to light a tea-light
      from the central candle (lit when the baby
      received her/his name), and say aloud what
      their hopes are for her/him.

17   *The ceremony is then ended with the cutting*
      of the cake, and a party.

The flower circlet can be dried, preserved and framed, along with the poems or extracts offered by the parents, if wished.

Birthing Celebrations for New Parents

Celebrations for parents are wholly different to that for the baby, as the parents are entering a new phase of their lives now, especially with the arrival of a first child. As with the ritual above, using the word 'parents' here does not imply that this is the 'norm' or the ideal in any way. This is a ceremony that can be celebrated by same-sex parents, or a single parent, whether male or female.

This type of ceremony, in direct contrast to the one above, is set in private, as it is more likely that the parent/s will want to mark what this event in their lives means to them and, if a couple, to their relationship with each other. It may mark a change in roles, and this can mean one or the other leaving work to take care of the child during the other's working hours, or changing work schedules in order to co-parent effectively. What is important is that birthing celebrations for new parents should acknowledge such changes in a way that makes sense within their lives. This, of course, offers an opportunity otherwise denied most new parents, of specifically stating to each other what those roles are going to be, rather than resting on the assumption of how the other feels, or what society impresses upon them.

The form of such a ritual, of course, should be decided by the people in question. This could consist, possibly, of a simple circle, with two candles in the centre, and a couple facing each other, stating what their hopes and fears are, how they feel, and asking for the blessing of an appropriate Goddess for their new role as a parent. Ideal patron Goddesses of parenthood are Isis, Juno, Demeter, Modron and Rhiannon. Other Goddesses may express different aspects of parenting, such as Vesta, as patron of the safe home, Frigg, Goddess of the hearth and home crafts, or even Sekhmet, as a fierce lioness and protector.

Handfasting, Marriage and Partnerships

Declaring one's partnership with another, in most cultures, leads to marriage. This is often not the case if the couple in question are gay or lesbian, however. For heterosexual couples there are also difficulties — either they may not belong to any religion offering a marriage ceremony, or they may feel that secular services are too perfunctory. It may also be the case that, where legal marriage is allowed, the implications present in the convention of marriage in that culture is not agreeable to the couple.

In Goddess spirituality, and indeed in some other forms of spirituality, such as Paganism or Wicca (a modern type of witchcraft), there is an alternative format for the joining together of a couple, known as 'handfasting'. This has quite a long history and is believed to have originated in Scotland, where a 'common-law' marriage, at least as it was popularly understood, took place by the public clasping of hands, and jumping over a broomstick together. This gave rise to the old expression for a non-legally-married couple living together as *'living over the brush'*. In one sense, it is a form of marriage — it is about a couple getting together, sharing a household, and declaring it to their family and friends. In another sense, it is not *conventional* marriage, which allows some couples to keep their relationship clearly different from that expected within the customs of marriage in mainstream society. Largely speaking, this is to avoid sexist assumptions about couples' domestic and private arrangements. On the other hand, some couples like to have the handfasting, and still do the 'legal thing' as a legal security shortcut.

One of the other distinctions of handfasting is that you have the choice of making it 'for life', or 'for as long as love lasts'. The latter is probably the most realistic, and this is not to be cynical, or wishing anyone's relationship ill! Love can last forever — if it does, all well and good. If it doesn't — it seems pretty sad to have to break a promise as well as break up the relationship. There is a Pagan tradition that states that a handfasting can be for *'a year and a day'*. This gives couples a get-out clause, and a chance to see if they wish to renew their promises to each other. Some couples, therefore, decide to have a private ceremony the first time, then go public when they decide to renew after the year-and-a-day in question.

Below is a typical ritual outline for a handfasting ceremony. Like all the rituals described in this book, this is not definitive, but simply a framework that can be adapted, altered or even rejected, according to preference. The ritual outlined below, however, is a typical Goddess-centred handfasting ceremony. This one calls upon

Aphrodite and Vesta to represent love, passion and domestic harmony — some people may disagree with this choice, and the couple should select the Goddesses they deem most meaningful to their ceremony.

Handfasting Ceremony

Prior to the ceremony, you should arrange for a couple of friends or family members to agree to carry out the offices for bread and wine. In addition, you will need to choose which poems or extracts you want read, and select songs you want played. Favourite readings sometimes come from Kahlil Gibran, or ancient blessings. Whatever you choose, they should reflect what you wish to say about your choice to be together, and be about love or partnership, or perhaps your favourite song (provided it is suitable to the occasion!). You may wish to decorate the ritual space with flowers and candles, especially if you are holding the ceremony indoors. If you are holding the ceremony outside, you will need to choose somewhere reasonably undisturbed, yet accessible enough for friends and relatives to attend. Most handfasting invitations stipulate that people can wear what they like, but dress colourfully. Clothing is really a matter of choice, as is the decision to film or photograph the actual ceremony — or not. As ever, the Element candles should be set up around the circle, equidistant from each other.

You Will Need

Personnel
A couple!
Elements Officers for Air, Fire, Water, Earth and Spirit
An Officer for Bread

An Officer for Wine or Juice

Ingredients
Element candles
Rose or patchouli incense stick
A silken cord, preferably purple
A loaf of bread

Readers

A ring-bearer

Wine or juice, poured into
a chalice or wine glass
Rings and ring-cushion
Broomstick

1 *Light incense.*

2 *The Element Officer for Air should light the
Air candle, saying:*

May the Goddess of wisdom and insight
fill your days and bring you the gifts of
communication, reasoning and memory, so
that you will always speak with each other,
see good sense, and gather memories to
cherish.

3 *The Element Officer for Fire should light the
Fire candle, saying:*

May the Goddess of light and warmth fill
your days and bring you the gifts of passion,
courage and joy, so that you will always love
bravely and be happy.

4 *The Element Officer for Water should light the
Water candle, saying:*

May the Goddess of love and harmony
fill your days and bring you the gifts of
affection, balance and wholeness, so that
you will always follow your hearts, in
wisdom and in health.

5 *The Element Officer for Earth should light the Earth candle, saying:*

May the Goddess of plenty fill your days and bring you the gifts of food, shelter and enough to share with friends, so that you will always eat, drink and be merry!

6 *The Element Officer for Spirit should light the Spirit candle, saying:*

May the Goddess of connection fill your days and bring you the gifts of connection and transformation, so that you will always grow in each other's care, and be willing to accept change.

7 *One of the couple should then welcome the guests to their ceremony:*

In this space, and in this company, [partner's name] and I have come to make our commitment to each other.

The other partner should then go on:

[Partner's name] and I are happy to have you here to take part in our handfasting, which is our way of saying to each other, our family and friends that we love each other and want to be together.

8   *At this point, a reading chosen by the couple should be made to the company by one of their friends.*

9   *The Officer for bread should present the couple with a loaf of bread, saying:*

May you never want for bread, or life's necessities.

10   *The Officer for water should present the couple with the wine or juice, saying:*

May you never thirst for beauty by finding it in each other.

11   *At this point, a song, chosen by the couple, should be played.*

12   *The ring-bearer should come forward with the rings on a cushion, and wait whilst the couple exchange their promises.*

13   *Partner one should take the ring from the cushion, and holding the other's ring hand, ask:*

[Partner's name], will you accept this ring, a symbol of love and trust, as a token of the love we are declaring in this circle and before this company?

259

Will you accept me as your partner, to live together and share what life brings?

When the other answers Yes *the ring should be placed on the finger. Then partner two should go through the same process. The ring-bearer should leave the circle at this point, and a broom should be placed across the path of the couple.*

14   *Partner one should pick up the silken cord and with the help of partner two, they should tie it around the wrists of their respective ring-hands.*

15   *At this point, a second reading, chosen by the couple, should be made to the company by one of their friends.*

16   *Partner one should turn to partner two and say:*

I ask Aphrodite, Goddess of love, to bless our union and remind us of how much we love each other today, years in the future.

Partner two should respond to partner one by saying:

I ask the Goddess Vesta, Goddess of the hearth, to bless our union and bring harmony and comfort to our home.

17   *At this point, a second song, chosen by the*
     couple, should be played.

18   *Both partners should now move towards the*
     broomstick and, facing each other, say to one
     another in turn:

     [Partner's name], will you be my partner, my
     lover and my friend?

     Will you travel with me and keep me
     company on the journey?

     Shall we be shelter for each other, a comfort
     when the path is rocky?

     Shall we support each other, and rejoice
     when the path is smooth?

     Shall we be honest and kind with each
     other?

     Shall we be courageous and allow each to
     grow and change?

     Shall we be generous and remember the
     good in each other?

19   *In answer to these questions, the couple*
     should jump, hand in hand over the broom-
     stick. The handfasting is then complete.

Death, Funerals and Memorials

One of the joys of do-it-yourself ceremonies is the freedom with which one can construct such rituals. In the case of funeral and memorial rituals, this is doubly so, as sometimes such ceremonies are presided over by people who did not know the deceased person, and have injected into them sentiments that the deceased, in life, would have baulked at. This can be distressing and annoying for mourners who may be feeling that they wish to do their best for their dead friend, and remember her/him as they would wish to be remembered. Of course, one of the down-sides of do-it-yourself ceremonies is that at times of shock, grief and distress it is usually easier to retreat into known litany than to construct something wholly new. This is a problem that many Pagans and other Goddess people have come to recognize, and have worked at resolving over the last few years.[1] What some members of the community have done is to construct a framework for funerals and memorial services, and publish them,[2] or post them on the internet.

Passing from life into death is seen, in Goddess spirituality, as a process, not a final end-moment in our existence. Whatever we believe happens to the spirit or soul of a person (if indeed we believe in souls) after death, we recognize that the person who has died has left a legacy that ensures they live on. If they have children, they live on in them, and as long as they live in the loving memory of another person, or the impact of their actions continues to flow outwards into the web, then some part of them lives on. We also recognize that the grieving of those left behind is important as a part of the process of their healing, and as a way of remembering the dead. This process is often recognized by fixing a memorial service approximately three moons after the actual funeral (burial or cremation). By this time, people, though still grieving, are not so much in shock as they were at a funeral ritual, and have had time to gather their thoughts about how they remember their friend. Memorial services, then, honour not only the dead, but the feelings and needs of the living.

One way of saving family and friends the painful task of putting together a funeral ritual at a time when they are in shock, and feeling less than creative, is to leave a record of your preferences for a funeral — even to the point of copying down a ritual from a book or the internet, and specifying what music you would wish played, or readings made, if any. This is not morbid — it is commonsense and a kindness to your family and friends. It is not over-controlling either — friends could get a chance to express themselves in a later memorial service, and you could indicate that you would like this to happen, too.

Goddesses associated with death include Hecate, Morrigan, and the Cailleach, or 'Old Woman'. One associated with passing over into death, and often mentioned at Goddess-centred funerary rites, is Rhiannon, perhaps because of her association with the sea, over which, in the western parts of the British Isles, the dead were said to pass. Most commonly, the *sweet birds of Rhiannon* are invoked to carry the dead one to their rest. Depending upon the tradition, sometimes the Triple Goddess of healing, thought to have carried King Arthur away to Avalon, is invoked, to carry away those who have died either from violence or disease. In other traditions, Nephthys, Queen of mystery and magic, and one of the four Goddesses of the dead, is invited to carry away the spirit of the dead one.

Which Goddess is invoked, and which image of death is used, is very much dependent upon the individual whose death is being marked, and the understanding of the ritual participants who are left to mourn. This being the case, it makes perfect sense to write down your wishes and make it clear to your nearest and dearest that you have written down your preferences and lodged them somewhere that they can be accessed in case of death. Don't be dismayed if your family recoil, or even find it amusing — people react oddly sometimes to the thought of death, and would rather pretend that it isn't going to happen. It is really considerate to your loved ones to have things in hand should you die suddenly, and not at all selfish to be specific about it. If you have done your research on burial and cremation laws and regulations, and have some knowledge of sites where you can have the funeral of your choice, including woodlands that are specifically set aside for environmentally-friendly funerals, so much the better for them! But do be prepared for a reaction of denial, or embarrassment — these seem very common, even if death is one of the very few things we can absolutely depend upon to happen!

Exercise: Funeral Ceremony

Now that you have had a chance to read about Goddess-centred understandings of life and death, and have seen some basic ritual frameworks for other occasions, you should be able to construct a simple funeral ceremony for yourself. You may need to do a little research in the books mentioned in the recommended reading section, or surf the internet, but this book has given you enough basic understanding of Goddess beliefs and rituals to enable you to construct your own. Using your notebook, then, see if you can construct a funeral ceremony that you would wish to have performed at your funeral. There are no definitive answers, so this exercise can only be judged by yourself; you may wish to return from time to time to the notebook to refine your ideas and preferences, which may well change over time.

In the meantime, you may wish to consider the following points:

- *Who could you trust to leave the instructions with?*

- *Are your requirements strictly realistic? (Being buried in the middle of Richmond Park or burned on a pyre in your favourite beauty spot is probably not.)*

- *Is there likely to be resistance to your wishes? If so, you may need to talk to a few people about them, so that they are clear.*

- *Which Goddesses would you wish invoked?*

- *Do you have an image of Death that you can use to help you write your funeral plans? (ie is it appropriate to speak of 'crossing over', 'passing through' or 'being reborn'?)*

- *Is there enough space in the funeral for participants, rather than just one person, offering a recitation or reading?*

- *Does the order of your ceremony make sense?*

- *Do you want music, a party or something unusual to help people remember you, and are these realistic requests?*

- *Are you covered by any insurance, or do you have any money tucked away for your requests? Remember, it is very selfish to leave requests that family and friends then feel duty-bound to pay for.*

265

Growing Up: Wo/manhood

We live in a society that does not really have any rites of passage for young becoming-women and becoming-men. Certainly the first mark of young womanhood, menstruation, is still virtually taboo in much of western society, and young men, outside of Bar Mitzvahs and other religiously-specific celebrations, have very little to mark their passage into manhood.

It can be very difficult to mark this passage through puberty for young people in a society where womanhood and manhood have such prescribed, complementary meanings. A young woman is subject to all the pressures of ideologies of a particular type of femininity, and young men are subject to all the pressures of conforming to a certain type of masculinity. It doesn't have to be like this. Feminist households with daughters have, over the past 30 years, found different ways of celebrating the onset of the daughter's menstrual periods, including throwing a party for the young woman's friends, where everybody wears red or pink, and all foods offered are red! This is to emphasize that red is a powerful and positive colour, and that bleeding is not dirty or shameful, but something to be celebrated in high style! Some communities have found all-male sweat lodges to be an ideal rite of passage from boyhood to manhood, though it must be said that the values of 'masculinity' passed on at some of these occasions are extremely anti-feminist and highly questionable.

The social pressures on young people to conform, rather than be different, makes celebration of these important passages in their lives a little difficult at times — it must, after all, be the young person's choice. Having some sort of format, or suggestion to offer as to how to celebrate the changes they are going through, however, makes it easier for young people to value them. In the exercise that follows the next section, you will have an opportunity to explore this further, but another way of helping young people to see the value in the different stages of life, is also found in the way that we mark other rites of passage, including the processes that take us towards elderhood.

Growing Old: Crone/Elderhood

One of the processes undervalued in western society is that of ageing: in fact it is something many of us positively seek to avoid. This is due to a number of things, including a culture of youth, and an ideology that is linked to ideas of economic worth and productivity rather than the value of experience and the 'wealth' of wisdom. This is a sad state of affairs, and the disparagement and anti-value attached to old age are also somewhat unrealistic — in the normal run of things, we are all going to experience growing older. It is true that not everyone grows wise as they grow older — some people can just keep on making the same mistakes and offer bad advice. But this is the case with younger people, too, and their contribution to society is not devalued because of this.

Goddess people are acutely aware of the way in which our society fetishes youth at the expense of valuing elderhood. If elderhood is part of our natural life-cycle, then it is of equal value to all other stages of that cycle. Like these other stages, it brings different gifts with it, which can be positively valued. These include the physical changes that in mainstream society are dreaded, or even mocked, such as lines, wrinkles, grey hair, cessation of menstrual bleeding and/or slowing down of the sexual functions in both men and women.

When we examine these changes more closely, it becomes apparent there is no need for any of these physical changes to be dreaded. The lines and wrinkles in our faces and on our bodies are marks of the experiences of laughter and sorrow, that have helped us to be who we are in old age. They are also the consequences of walking for so many years on the planet. The stretch marks and lines on the bark of a tree are not mocked; they are simply part of the tree that bears the mark of its genus, its life story, and contains within it the secrets of the tree's growth. How absurd, then, that humans subject to the perfectly natural process of ageing are subject to other people's projections of their own dread of old age! The coming of grey hairs is so dreaded in western society that there are special products on the market to 'hide' them. And yet, there is a world of beauty in a head of grey hair that is not just about valuing older people, but about aesthetic appreciation. There are so many shades of grey and white seen in older people's hair — slate, blue, silver, white, that are simply not appreciated. This is not to say that there is anything wrong in trying to look your best — it is about choices about how you wish to value yourself, and having those choices respected.

One of the ways in which elderhood can be celebrated is by having a Croning or Elderhood ceremony. Croning ceremonies have become particularly popular among older women in the US; these are ways of helping women, who are particularly subject to sexism and ageism, to value the gifts they bring with them into their elderhood. For women, valued in patriarchy only as mothers or 'lookers', old age implies a loss of attractiveness, and the end of the reproductive function. This leaves women very little, according to these ideologies, once they hit the menopause. But beauty is very relative, as older women discover, to who is defining it and seeking it out. Goddess spirituality challenges all forms of discrimination, including that of ageism, so there is plenty of scope for discovering alternative forms of beauty and worth to those defined by patriarchal capitalism. These are not, in fact, hard to find. A Croning ceremony offers ways of recognizing and affirming all the gifts of old age, and allows women to celebrate with friends the end of one life-stage and the beginning of another. At these rituals, women have the opportunity to express their feelings about the different periods of their lives that they have been through and occasionally the relief they feel at leaving these behind! Recognizing the beauty of old age is also a part of this, and confirms not only to the woman herself, but to the people in attendance, the continuing and different worth of a woman passing into an important part of her life — a period into which she has been growing for the whole extent of that life.

For men, elderhood is a period that mainstream society also dismisses. In a patriarchal, capitalist society that values men's roles as workers, and biological rather than supportive fatherhood, old age is considered a time of non-production. The 'bread-winner' identity, always precarious and oppressive, is stripped away and this often leaves men feeling useless. Even pro-feminist and politically-aware men suffer from the comments of colleagues and friends as they retire. The implication of 'impotence', in terms of sexual function is also underlined by the implications of lack of economic 'virility', and this 'double whammy' is politically and personally undermining. An Elderhood celebration, then, can help men to regain definition of who and what is important in their lives, in a space outside of the fears and inaccuracies attached to images of old men in mainstream society.

A Croning party is usually attended by women only, though this is very much the choice of the woman herself. Like an Elderhood celebration, this may be something that the person concerned may wish to restrict to Elders only. However, there is a great deal to be said for the virtues of example and demonstration, so inviting younger people and allowing them into some of the secrets of elder beauty and wisdom is probably good, positive PR for Elderhood!

Exercise: Celebrating the Coming of Wo/Manhood and/or Elderhood

Section A

The two previous sections have raised issues of importance to those celebrating their Elderhood (or Cronehood, if women prefer!), and the difficulties of celebrating the coming of wo/manhood in young people. If you were planning a ritual for entering womanhood or Cronehood for a friend, which Goddesses would you call upon to be the patrons of the ceremony for entering womanhood, respectively? Write these down in your notebook, with a note of why you think they are suitable for the rites of passage to which you have assigned them. You may wish to cover up Section B below so that you can focus on attempting your own answers. You may also find it helpful to refer back to the section in chapter two that discussed links between the life-cycle of the Goddess and that of humans, and to revisit the glossary of Goddesses in chapter three.

Section B

As ever, the answers below are only possibilities, and you can measure your own against them, to see if you have considered all possibilities.

Firstly, possible patrons for a ritual to celebrate a young woman's first menstruation:

Lilith	Because of Her associations with the moon and the menstrual cycle.

Selene	Again, because She is a moon Goddess, whose symbol is the face of the full moon, which occurs, like women's bleeding, once in the month.
Diana	Especially for an all-female gathering, as She is the patron of the sisterhood of women.
Maia, Bloddueth or Persephone	All Goddesses of Spring, which in terms of the human life-cycle, is the blossoming into womanhood.
Demeter and Persephone	As a supportive, mother-daughter pair, symbolizing the mutual support amongst women, and the coming of a daughter into womanhood.
Ceridwen	Because of her symbol the cauldron, felt by many Goddess women to be a particularly female symbol of life, creativity and regeneration, the possibilities of which are realized in the young becoming-woman, and in the life-cycle generally.

Next, possible patrons for a ceremony to celebrate a woman's Cronehood (known as a 'Croning'):

Annis	Because She is a keeper of wisdom and arcane knowledge.
Baubo	A crone Goddess of laughter and the wisdom of ridiculing that which is absurd and superficial — a gift of old age!

Ceridwen	In her Hag aspect, an old, wise witch who can shape-shift and outwit the cleverest of humans.
Sophia	Goddess of wisdom.
Danu	Wise and loving protector of the people and the land.
Grandmother Spider	The wise story-weaver and patron of transformation.

You may have had alternative suggestions, with explanations that satisfy you of your choice. This is fine; what matters is that you can think your way around the symbols and associations of the Goddesses and apply this practically and appropriately.

Exercise: Celebrating Your Place in the Life-Cycle

Now that you have had a practice run on sorting out patron Goddesses for different life-changes, you should find it easier to plan a ritual for your own stage in the journey. Earlier, in chapter two, you were invited to consider which point of your life-cycle you have reached. The point you have reached does not have to be specifically any of the ones mentioned above, ie entering wo/manhood or elderhood, indeed, these in themselves are a long process. Simply try to work out where you are. You may like to cover the guidance notes in Section B while you are considering the task set out in Section A.

Section A

1   *When you have noted down, as best you can,
    your current position in your life-cycle, write
    underneath all the Goddesses you think would
    be good patrons for a ceremony to celebrate
    this part of your journey.*

2   *Using a process of elimination, reduce your
    list to just three, and see if you can name
    which aspects of your present place in the
    life-cycle they respectively represent.*

3   *Write yourself a private, solo ceremony to
    celebrate this point of your natural lifespan,
    jotting down a skeleton outline of the ritual.*

Section B

1   *Remember to check back in the glossary in
    chapter three, carrying out a little more
    background research in books in the
    recommended reading section and on the
    internet, and meditate upon your choices
    before decide which three Goddesses to invite
    to your life-cycle ceremony.*

2   *Whilst planning a ritual, you should
    remember the practical elements, such as
    which symbols, colours, candles and incenses
    are needed, and whether these are affordable
    and easily accessible in the time-span you
    have allotted yourself.*

3   *Your ritual framework should probably have
all of the following elements:*

*Casting of the circle, or declaration of sacred
space.*

*Welcoming Elements, possibly with a speech
specific to the ceremony at hand.*

*Welcoming the three Goddesses you have
chosen, and saying something of their
attributes, and why they are appropriate
patrons of your celebration.*

*Some form of divination for the next stage in
your life, ie tarot cards, runes, I-Ching coins, if
you are already adept at divining patterns
with these tools,* or *a planned inner journey
or meditation to receive guidance on the next
stage of your journey through life.*

*Some symbolic activity related to the things
you have left behind and the things you now
value about your life-cycle status! Choose
your symbols carefully, being clear with
yourself that they are appropriate.*

*A declaration of how you value the good
things that your present life-cycle status
offers you, and others, and a wish for the
strength and courage to continue to value
these things in yourself and in others.*

> *Some form of closure for the circle, or sacred space you have declared.*
>
> *Food and drink, to 'ground' yourself after the ritual.*

Exercise: Thinking about Rituals, Purpose and Planning

This section is intended to get you thinking about the possibilities offered by Goddess-centred rituals and ceremonies. Taking into account all that you have learned, in this chapter and in this book, about festivals, the cycles of nature, the alternative ways of interpreting the human life-cycle, and other important events, try to note down the different ways that you would like to mark these. Begin with birthdays, anniversaries, and the eight festivals and, when you are ready, move on to other events. All you have to do is to write under the heading of each possible reason for celebration, the answers to the following questions:

- *What is my main purpose in wishing to celebrate this event?*

- *Which Goddesses are most suited as patrons of this event?*

- *At which point of the year is this celebrated, and is it suitable for outdoor or indoor celebrations?*

- *Is this something I could celebrate alone, or should I invite friends?*

WAY of

- *If the latter, who should I invite to participate in the ritual?*

- *Would this ritual work best free-standing or as something surrounded by a party?*

- *If the latter, who should I invite to the party, and who should I ask to help me with the ritual part of the day/evening?*

- *Should I write a 'script' for me and my friends to memorize/read from, or should I consult with others taking part to see what they have to offer by way of planning the ritual?*

- *How could I symbolize the main aspects of this celebration?*

- *Which activities might be carried out in the course of this ceremony (ie cutting a cake, lighting candles and making declarations, using symbols and doing something relevant with them)?*

- *Should I have music, or will this be intrusive?*

- *How might I word my invocation of the Elements/the Goddess/es?*

- *How do I want to end this ritual?*

- *How much food and drink will be needed to pass around amongst guests at this ceremony?*

Provided that you bear all of these questions in mind, you should be able, from examples set out in this chapter, and elsewhere in the book, to plan and carry out your own rituals. May all of them be wonderful!

Notes

1   *Starhawk, 1997.*
2   *Ibid.*

TEN

WAY OF THE
Goddess

Now that you have read through this book, you should have a firm idea of what Goddess spirituality is about, and how it is different from other forms of spirituality. As you no doubt will have discovered for yourself, through the exercises, and the information found in the different chapters, Goddess spirituality is a life-affirming path, which seeks to celebrate our existence on this planet. In doing so, it also makes clear the choices we face in choosing how and why we celebrate, and offers alternatives to some of the rather limited and prescriptive choices that are offered within mainstream society and, to a certain extent, some mainstream religions. On our path, body, mind and spirit are considered equally as valid, and to be valued; we do not elevate spirit above body or mind. Our spirits and our spirituality are just another part of us, like skin, teeth, bones, abilities and attitudes. Goddess spirituality honours and values diversity, recognizes the wealth of experience and the richness of variety and places these above ideologies that, proverbially, know the price of everything and the value of nothing. We do not consider it 'bad' to have blessings, but unjust that some people do not, and seek to redress this in our actions as well as our sentiments. It is not a path of suffering — indeed, we try to work towards alleviating suffering. Goddess spirituality doesn't 'do' *guilt*, but it does 'do' *responsibility*!

If this is a path that you choose, you will be blessed indeed! It is not an easy path, any more than it is strewn with the thorns and rocks so beloved of some religious preferences; you will not be immune to life, but open to it. You will find sisters and brothers around the world who will recognize some part of your path and beliefs. You will find affinities and similarities between Goddess spirituality and other paths, such as Witchcraft and Paganism, as well as the interesting cross-fertilizations that have taken place between all three. You will also find a world-wide community of people who honour the Goddess, either in the form of different Goddesses, or as part of a religion that honours both Goddesses and Gods, and there are sometimes things to learn from all of these.

You should remember that not everyone who honours the Goddess in Her many forms will necessarily agree with your spiritual or political beliefs, or be feminist or even woman-friendly. After all, the ancient Greeks had Goddesses, but their society was extremely misogynistic! Research has shown that societies which elevate certain female icons often do so to denigrate ordinary women, and to keep the gendered order of society in place.[1] On the other hand, not being able to make assumptions is always a good spur to conversation and the exchange of new ideas!

Your Relationship to the Goddess Community

If this is the path for you, you will probably be interested in meeting some of the other hundreds of thousands of people who, like you, honour the Goddess. This book has introduced you to some basic beliefs, ideas and practices that are common in our community, so you will not be entering the domain of the Goddess community entirely ignorant of what to expect.

It may be that you want to work with others who are Goddess-centred, either as a working 'circle', or as a group that meets for regular Moon or festival circles, or as a Goddess discussion group. If you wish to learn more, it may be possible for you to find someone more experienced to be a mentor until you gain confidence in ritual and magical work. You may also wish to contact other people through workshops that are offered occasionally. I strongly advise those considering joining groups or going to workshops *not* to pay out huge sums of money for workshops, lessons or pledges to a group, or to pay heed to anyone who expects you to extend sexual favours. Unfortunately, there are some unscrupulous people out there, who are only too willing to take advantage of 'rookies' — though which spiritual path they *think* they are following is anybody's guess.

Although I do not, personally, ever charge for workshops, there are some perfectly honourable and genuine teachers who do charge a small fee, usually to reimburse their expenses and labour. The emphasis here, however, is on a *small* fee. There is a joke in the Pagan movement about the costs of workshops, and the difference between a Pagan and a New Age workshop is said to be a decimal point and several noughts! This applies to Goddess workshops, too, so bear this in mind when you are pricing up such events and deciding whether they are going to be worth attending. Naturally, as you encounter others, you will learn more, and come to trust your judgement about what sounds right to you, and what sounds suspect. But it is, understandably, difficult sometimes to judge when you are new to something, whether someone is really being straightforward with you. Ask the Wise Woman within what She thinks, and if you are still unsure, follow the old adage of *'If in doubt, don't!'*

If you do join a group, be vigilant early on to see if there are any signs of unhealthy over-reliance on a 'leader'. If there are, your group is probably not a healthy environment in which to explore your spiritual path. If there is a hierarchy, you are probably not in a Goddess group that has explored their awareness of balance and justice, and again, this is not going to be rich soil in which to grow self-awareness and spiritual understanding. The major thing to watch out for is the group that draws people in by the use of Goddess imagery, and lip-service to feminism, but turns around a leader whose declarations are not open to question. If there is an undue emphasis on a particular personality, and you are discouraged from disagreeing with decisions that are passed on to you, get out fast. Not all cults are necessarily harmful, but you are not going to find Goddess spirituality as it has been described in this book, in such an environment. It would be nice to think that everyone in the world can trust and learn from each other, but until the world changes somewhat, it remains just that; a nice thought. In the meantime, there are a number of highly reputable groups you could contact for information, or notification of workshops, and associations that can help you make contact with others. Some of these are broadly Pagan rather than specifically Goddess-centred, but can use their contacts to put you in touch with other Goddess-centred people. Some of these are listed in the Contacts section.

The Goddess in the Wider Community

While you are looking at your future as a member of the Goddess community, it is worth considering the role of the Goddess in the wider community, and what part of this role you may wish to play. Many Goddess people consider involvement in the local, regional, national, international and global human community an important part of their spiritual path and development. This community, remember, includes not only human affairs, but those of animals and nature. Many Goddess people concentrate on political change for humans, whilst others support change by working for the welfare of animals or the environment. Chapters five and six discussed the way in which we are all aspects of the Goddess, and invited you to write your Cosmic Job Description. Now is the time to act on that description, and be that part of the Goddess of Change who acts to promote justice and balance.

There are also other ways of bringing the Goddess into the wider community in a pro-active way: public rituals are a great way of raising public awareness of important issues. In the recent past, environmentalists have conducted public rituals on threatened land — a good way of making people aware of what is happening, and of what is at stake. Naturally, learning to work with a group is important here, as you will need to work with others to make the kind of impact required to grab public attention — and raise some powerful energy!

Bringing images of the Goddess into public space is also an important aspect of the Goddess in the wider community. Positive female imagery outside of the contexts of glamour and prescriptive 'beauty' are rare in patriarchal society, and Goddess-centred imagery offers women and men alike an alternative take on what it means to be female. Moreover, the addition of such images serve to beautify public space, which can so often be ugly. Placing Goddess images around us enables us to positively value ourselves, and help the Goddess reclaim what is Hers.

Looking Towards Your Future: Arhianrod's Mirror

Look into Arhianrod's mirror. This is the mirror of mysteries, that shows the past, the present and the future. Look into your future, and try to see yourself in five years' time. Ask yourself what you will be doing, what are your aspirations, your plans and your wishes for five years from now. How are planet Earth and her people doing, do you think? Now think about what you need to do in order to meet your aspirations and wishes, what plans you need to make, and how you intend to do something about planet Earth and Her people. The simple truth is that you can make a difference, to yourself, to others, and the state of the planet. What you do matters. So look into Arhianrod's mirror very often, whenever you need reminding of where you are going and what you are doing — Arhianrod resides within you, as well as within Her crystal tower, and She knows.

The Once and Future Goddess

Looking back over the millennia in which the Goddess, in some form or another, has existed, many things seem hard to believe, and some also seem contradictory. It seems hard to believe, for example, that She should have survived, given the power of patriarchy and its various attempts to destroy Her altogether. On the other hand, it seems hard to believe that, given the length of time over which the Goddess *has* survived, some people are still unaware of Her existence! Here we are, in the technologically-advanced twenty-first century, looking back at the ancient and prehistoric past to find clues and inspiration to take with us into the future, for our spiritual, intellectual and physical survival on this planet. Perhaps Grandmother Spider, and all the weaving Goddesses, for whom the past, the present and the future are all one, are chuckling away at our exclamations around such seeming contradictions, because they already know what the future holds.

Whatever it does hold, the journey of the Goddess over more than 30 millennia, from Her survival and, during the last century, from 'fertility idol', to spiritual and political focus in the personal development of women and men all over the world, has already been amazing. The Goddess community, developing and growing all the time, will play an important part in the next stage of the journey of humans, and the planet. On your journey, I wish you well, on *our* journey, I wish us all well. Blessed Be.

Blessing for one setting out on the path of the Goddess

Walk in the way of the Goddess
Walk in Her footsteps as She walks in yours

Notes

1   Raphael, in Griffin, 2000, page 97.

BIBLIOGRAPHY

Billington, S & Green, M (eds) (1996) *The Concept of the Goddess* Routledge: London.

Bottigheimer, RB (1987) *Grimms' Bad Girls and Bold Boys: The Moral and Social Vision of the Tales* Yale: New Haven & London.

Christ, CP (1995) *Diving Deep & Surfacing: Women Writers on Spiritual Quest* Beacon Press: Boston.

Christ, CP & Plaskow, J (eds) (1992) *Womanspirit Rising: A Feminist Reader in Religion* HarperCollins: San Francisco.

Clarissa Pinkola Estes (1992) *Women Who Run with the Wolves: Contacting the Power of the Wild Woman* Rider: London.

Griffin, W (ed) (2000) *Daughters of the Goddess: Studies of healing, Identity and Empowerment* AltaMira: New York.

Harvey, G (1997) *Listening People, Speaking Earth: Contemporary Paganism* Hurst & Co: London.

Harvey, G & Hardman, C (1996) *Paganism Today: Wiccans, Druids, the Goddess and Ancient Earth Traditions for the Twenty-First Century* Thorsons: London.

Hirshfield, J (ed) (1994) *Women in Praise of the Sacred: 43 Centuries of Spiritual Poetry by Women* HarperCollins: New York.

Hutton, R (1996) *The Stations of the Sun: A History of the Ritual Year in Britain* Oxford University Press: Oxford.

287

Hutton, R (2001) *The Triumph of the Moon: A History of Modern Pagan Witchcraft* Oxford University Press: Oxford.

Keller, Mara (1998) 'The interface of archaeology and mythology: the philosophical evaluation of the Gimbutas Paradigm', in *Pomegranate: A New Journal of NeoPagan Thought* Issue 5, August.

Larrington, C (ed) (1992) *The Feminist Companion to Mythology* Pandora: London.

Spretnak, C (1992) *Lost Goddesses of Early Greece: A Collection of Pre-Hellenic Myths* Beacon Press: Boston.

Starhawk, M Macha Nightmare and the Reclaiming Collective, (1997) *The Pagan Book of Living and Dying: Practical Rituals, Prayers, Blessings, and Meditations on Crossing Over* HarperCollins: San Francisco.

Walker, A (1988) *Living by the Word* The Women's Press, London.

Warner, M (1985) *Alone of all her sex: The myth and cult of the Virgin Mary* Picador: London.

RECOMMENDED
Reading

Many of the following also appear in the Bibliography — so come highly recommended. Others are suggested reading in relation to Goddess spirituality, though some include information on related paths such as Paganism. I heartily recommend that, if you choose to read any of the books from the following, you read with an open mind, but feel free to take the ideas that make sense, and leave behind those that do not. There is no reason why, because one idea in a philosophy appeals, you should have to take the whole philosophy on board, including those parts you find unappealing or nonsensical! Discernment in your early reading will serve you in good stead later on, and being selective is perfectly sensible. Happy Reading!

Adams, C (ed) (1991) *Ecofeminism and the Sacred* Continuum: NY.

Baring, A & Cashford, J (1991) *The Myth of the Goddess: Evolution of an Image* Viking: London.

Billington, S & Green, M (eds) (1996) *The Concept of the Goddess* Routledge: London.

Christ, CP & Plaskow, J (eds) (1992) *Womanspirit Rising: A Feminist Reader in Religion* HarperCollins: San Francisco.

Clarissa Pinkola Estes (1992) *Women Who Run with the Wolves: Contacting the Power of the Wild Woman* Rider: London.

Griffin, W (ed) (2000) *Daughters of the Goddess: Studies of Healing, Identity and Empowerment* AltaMira: New York.

Harvey, G (1997) *Listening People, Speaking Earth: Contemporary Paganism* Hurst & Co: London.

Hirshfield, J (ed) (1995) *Women in Praise of the Sacred: 43 Centuries of Spiritual Poetry by Women* HarperCollins: New York.

Larrington, C (ed) (1992) *The Feminist Companion to Mythology* Pandora: London.

Mor, B & Sjoo, M (1987) *The Great Cosmic Mother: Rediscovering the Religion of the Earth* Harper & Row: San Francisco.

Mountainwater, S (1996) *Ariadne's Thread: A Workbook of Goddess Magic* The Crossing Press: Freedom, CA.

Spretnak, C (1992) *Lost Goddesses of Early Greece: A Collection of Pre-Hellenic Myths* Beacon Press: Boston.

Starhawk, M Macha Nightmare and the Reclaiming Collective, (1997) *The Pagan Book of Living and Dying: Practical Rituals, Prayers, Blessings, and Meditations on Crossing Over* HarperCollins: San Francisco.

Starhawk (1981) *The Spiral Dance: A rebirth of the ancient religion of the Great Goddess* Harper SanFrancisco.

Walker, A (1987) *Living by the Word* Women's Press: New York.

CONTACTS

Whether you are looking out for local Goddess study groups, or a circle to work with, getting in contact is now made reasonably easy by internet links, and national and international organizations who have the means of keeping a list of networking contacts. You can, of course, always look out for posted contact messages on noticeboards in libraries, community centres or alternative cafes. However, sometimes internet searches turn up more information and useful links prior to actual contact, giving you more information upon which to decide whether you are interested, or whether the group concerned is suitable for your needs.

The following are contacts that are either Goddess-centred themselves, or can put you in touch with Goddess-centred groups. Many of these are contactable over the internet, and have links on their own web pages, so www. addresses are given wherever possible.

Circle PO Box 219, Mount Horeb, WI 53572, USA — www.circle-sanctuary.org. A pagan organization linked to a sacred site known as the Circle Sanctuary. Earth- and Goddess-friendly group.

Covenant of the Goddess, PO Box 1226, Berkeley, CA 94704, USA — www.cog.org. This is a Wiccan organization, which is a federation of covens, groups and individuals. The website is truly international, and includes UK, US and Australian contacts.

Dragon, 23b Pepys Road, New Cross, London, SE14 5SA — www.gn.apc.org/dragon, email Adrian@gn.apc.org. A network for eco-magic which is pro-feminist and Goddess-friendly. A good contact point for finding out about environmental campaigns and magical initiatives, and highly recommended.

House of the Goddess — www.hogonline.freeuk.com — is a London-based group, whose web page has lots of information about courses and literature. The site includes a Goddess Studies page, which is highly recommended.

Goddessing — www.goddessing.com. A bi-annual international Goddess research newspaper with contributions by some of the foremost scholars and writers on Goddess spirituality. Subscriptions to the newspaper are available from PO Box 269, Valrico, FL 33595, US, or PO Box 75, Sliema, Malta. Their website has a link with Goddess arts, crafts and bookshops. Highly recommended.

Pagan Federation BM Box 7079, London WC1N 3XX, UK — www.paganfed.demon.co.uk. The Pagan Federation is not an exclusively Goddess-centred organization, but does have a wide range of contacts in Britain that enable it to recommend Goddess-centred groups in your locality — if you ask nicely! For international links, the *Pagan Federation International* is at PO Box 473, Zeist, Nederlands NL 3700 AL, — www.paganfederation.org. The international branch website has lots of interesting worldwide links.

Reclaiming, PO Box 14404, San Francisco, CA 94114, USA — www.webcom.com/cauldron/. A feminist and pro-feminist collective, run along non-hierarchical lines, and adept at linking spirituality and politicality. Highly recommended first contact point with a good website.

Wood and Water is a feminist, Goddess-centred magazine which includes listings for events and contacts, including Goddess study courses and groups. They do not have a website, but can be contacted c/o Daniel Cohen, 77 Parliament Hill, London NW3 2TH.